The River Cottage

Hedgerow Handbook

The River Cottage
Hedgerow Handbook

by John Wright

introduced by

Hugh Fearnley-Whittingstall

www.rivercottage.net

B L O O M S B U R Y
LONDON · NEW DELHI · NEW YORK · SYDNEY

For my girls – Diane, Flossie and Lily

First published in Great Britain 2010

Text and photography © 2010 by John Wright

The moral right of the author has been asserted

Bloomsbury Publishing Plc, 50 Bedford Square, London WC1B 3DP

www.bloomsbury.com

Bloomsbury is a trademark of Bloomsbury Publishing Plc

Bloomsbury Publishing, London, New Delhi, New York and Sydney

A CIP catalogue record for this book is available from the British Library

ISBN 978 1 4088 0185 7

10 9 8 7 6

Project editor: Janet Illsley
Designer: willwebb.co.uk

Printed and bound in Italy by Graphicom

www.bloomsbury.com/rivercottage

Contents

Starting Out   8

Conservation and the Law   20

Edible Species   30

Poisonous Species   166

Recipes   198

Useful Things   244

Index   251

This is not the first time I've taken up my pen to introduce a book written by John Wright. I did so back in 2007, when John produced the very first River Cottage Handbook, *Mushrooms*, and I did it again a couple of years later when he wrote another, *Edible Seashore*. So to find myself musing on his work is not a novel experience, although it is one filled with pleasure and admiration. It's clear to me that there really is no limit to this man's enthusiasm and excitement about the great outdoors – the edible bits of it in particular. And this compact manual is just like its forerunners: erudite, authoritative, confidence-building, witty. It will tell you all you need to know to turn any little walk or ramble into a foraging expedition, and it will inspire and entertain you at the same time.

Foraging is, and has long been, a great timeless, life-enhancing pursuit. It is deeply satisfying, deeply grounding. It gets us out into the fresh air and brings us closer to the natural environment from which we can so easily become estranged. It's a lovely thing to do on your own and often even more fun if you get your family or a group of friends to join in. There are, of course, a few serious foraging dangers in the form of poisonous plants, but most perils are fairly minor... the odd nettle sting and the occasional muddy trousers, perhaps.

However, for me there is a certain risk attached to foraging when it is performed *à deux* – especially when I am one part of the *deux* and John is the other. Because, while foraging really shouldn't be a competitive sport, with John around, it becomes so at times. The pair of us don't seem to be able to resist seeing who can gather the greatest number of nuts, the hardest-to-reach damsons, or the rarest bit of edible greenery. For me, I suppose it's a chance to prove myself, to enhance my foraging street-cred. For John... well, I think it's just showing off.

But don't let our rivalries deter you from engaging in your own foraging adventure. Antler-locking is absolutely not an essential part of wild food gathering. It should be neither a race nor a contest, but simply a highly enjoyable, very productive pastime. What's more, foraging is something that can be done by almost anyone, almost anywhere. You don't need a four-wheel-drive vehicle, waders, orienteering skills or a plethora of specially shaped sticks to be able to gather some of your own wild food. As John has said on many previous occasions, 'You're never more than five minutes from a patch of nettles,' a phrase I think he poached from *A Cook on the Wild Side*. The strength of this book is that it brings home this accessibility.

What John also celebrates so marvellously is the sheer joy of the hunt. 'Finding one's own food is such a fundamental drive,' he says, 'it is unsurprising that it is so much fun – nature has a delightful tendency to reward us for doing things that are essential for life, but which are hard work, complex or even absurd.' I couldn't have put it better myself (though that won't stop me from trying).

John's approach is egalitarian and inclusive and he makes the point that we are all hunter-gatherers at heart. It may be the case that most of us don't do much hunting or gathering any more, but that doesn't mean we can't. His view – and mine too – is that 'instincts do not disappear just because we do not use them'. What's more, freed from any urgent necessity to find food for ourselves in the wild, we can now enjoy the search all the more. The hedgerow is perhaps the most accessible and least daunting type of wild food environment. Few of us are very far from some kind of woodland, field edge, heathland, allotment or, indeed, garden, and these habitats are all included in John's 'hedgerow' bracket. And, just to encourage you a little more, plant identification in these areas is generally more straightforward and less nerve-racking than in the world of, say, fungi.

One of the many things I love about John is the sheer relish he displays for consuming his wild harvest. He never loses sight of the fact that, at the end of the day, once you've filled your lungs with fresh air and put roses in your cheeks, foraging is about getting something good to eat. What you do with your booty once you get it home is very important and John is no less an expert on this than he is on finding it in the first place. He shares my view that simple dishes are, almost without exception, the best ones for wild food. From a simple Nettle Soup to a stunningly refreshing Watermint Sorbet and excellent Chestnut Florentines (a personal favourite of mine), the recipes alone will have you itching to don your wellies and start hunting.

However, should the weather, minor illness or some other misfortune curtail your foraging efforts at any point, you needn't be too disappointed. For this book, like all John's work, is so beautifully and entertainingly written that there's as much enjoyment to be had from reading it curled up on the sofa as under a tree or beside a stream. It's a book that I know will stay on my shelf well beyond the day when I have to hang up my boots and confine myself to armchair foraging permanently. I take every opportunity to rib John about the fact that this point of retirement is considerably further off for me than it is for him. But I sometimes wonder about that. As this piece of work testifies, wild food finding is in John's very blood and I imagine he'll be tramping his way along the hedgerows, basket at the ready and stick in hand, for many, many years to come. I certainly hope so.

Hugh Fearnley-Whittingstall, East Devon, June 2010

Starting Out

I am frequently told that going on a walk with me can be rather disconcerting. Except for the occasions when I offer my companion the odd leaf to chew upon, I appear to be strangely distracted and barely listening to what is being said to me. Well, I am – usually – listening; it is just that I am doing something else as well – looking.

Once one learns the foraging way of life, it is difficult to stop. Every walk, every car or train journey is an opportunity to find a new patch of Watermint, a likely spot for Pignuts or a promising-looking wood. If my walking is absent-minded, my driving is lethal. Foraging at 50mph, with eyes darting left and right and the occasional abrupt punctuations of the forager's emergency stop, has made me a danger to all road-users.

I hope that you come to love foraging and learning about foraging as much as I do. I know for certain that you will enjoy the food you find on your travels – eating wild Raspberries on a summer evening, for example, is difficult to beat. While many of the foods here are wild versions of familiar plants, there are several which may be new to you. Pignuts, Brooklime, Bulrush shoots and Silverweed roots are not readily found at even the best of greengrocers and are delicacies available only to the forager. Of course, there was a time when life was quite different, a time when there were no shops, no farms to supply them and not even a garden.

Ten or eleven thousand years ago in the Near East, not far from the mythical Garden of Eden, human beings made their greatest ever innovation: agriculture. For all the aeons before this, there was only one way our ancestors could obtain food – from the wild. Agriculture has been the backbone of our civilisation, relieving us of the time-consuming and unreliable daily hunt for food, but it has also deprived us of one of life's great pleasures.

While gathering wild food is still a matter of everyday life in many rural parts of the developed world (though much less so in Britain), nowadays the culture of hunting and foraging persists for most people largely as a pale remnant. Hunting has become a formalised and often ritualised sport; the true purpose, acquiring food, frequently forgotten. And few people now will forage for much more than a basket of Blackberries or a bag of Elderflowers. But, of course, instincts do not disappear just because we do not need them as we once did. Most of us now sublimate our foraging urges in supermarket aisles, which have been cunningly designed by Machiavellian retail psychologists to mimic the ancient experience.

Given that finding one's own food is such a fundamental drive, it is unsurprising that it is so much fun – nature has a delightful tendency to reward us for doing things that are essential for life but which are hard work, complex or even absurd. I take people out every year on various forays and it is wonderful to see their primal delight; all other concerns and thoughts flee and the single-minded nature of the enterprise becomes almost meditative.

With the need to find food in the wild no longer pressing, and most people living in an urban environment, the knowledge of what can be eaten, and where and when to find it, is no longer learned at a mother's side. Books can tell you the 'what' and to a large extent the 'when', but the 'where' cannot be described beyond generalities. The precise location of particular plants was knowledge passed down through the generations; Pignuts are always found *here* and there is a plum tree *here*, *here* and *here*, with the second one producing the best fruit. Such things now have to be learned anew. I have a mental map of exactly where hundreds of different wild foods can be found and a sense of my chances on any particular day, but this is hard-earned knowledge acquired from years of searching – if my mother knew where to find Pignuts she has kept the information to herself.

This book won't tell you exactly where to find Pignuts either, but I hope it will fill in some of the gaps and point you more or less in the right direction. As your life no longer depends on knowing where to find wild food, you have the leisure to enjoy the search, with every new discovery an exciting one. Coming across an unsuspected woodland clearing full of ripe Raspberries or a Chestnut tree producing good-sized nuts is a wonderful experience.

There is so much to enjoy here and I hope you will become the hunter/gatherer you were designed to be.

Where to look

The title of this book is 'Hedgerow' but it actually covers plants found in many more places than this. Wood, mountainside, moor, bog, heath, stream, meadow, field edge, seashore, urban wasteland, garden and allotment can all produce an abundance of wild foods. Most people can make a good start by looking in their own flower-beds – Hairy Bittercress, Dandelion, Ground Elder, Silverweed and Corn Salad can all be found in the average flower garden and it is rather satisfying to be able to eat your weeds. The vegetable garden can supply even finer delicacies, such as Fat Hen and Spear-leaved Orache.

One of my favourite spots for foraging is other people's veg patches and I am something of a familiar figure at the local allotments. There was some suspicion at first from the gardeners, but when my requests to pick some of their weeds proved *not* to be a cover for theft or sabotage, I was welcomed as a harmless idiot. In fact, few places are more packed with wild edible greens than the disturbed ground of an allotment garden – with Fat Hen, Spear-leaved Orache, Red Goosefoot and Chickweed available by the sackful. You may not be quite so lucky as I am – some allotments have fallen under the firm hand of an officious parish clerk or allotment association and will be scrupulously weed free. Also, the organic revolution has not touched the hearts and souls of all who practise horticulture, so the patch of Fat Hen you have been eyeing up for the last week may have recently been sprayed with 2,4-Dichlorophenoxyacetic acid or something equally unappetising. Always check with your friendly gardener first.

Even without the wildlife refuge of many gardens, the urban forager need not feel left out. Around twenty species mentioned in this book are commonly found in odd corners of our cities and suburbs. Fennel, Perennial Wall Rocket, Rowan, Blackberry, Stinging Nettle, Wild Strawberry and others are all as much, or even more, at home in town as out. Not that urban foraging is without its perils. Herbicidal sprays, pollution and, most of all, dogs, can make a forage around town a dicey business. There is good news though: pollution from motor vehicles is not what it was when lead was an ingredient in petrol. All that lead has now been washed away and is, mercifully, not being replenished. Other fuel and exhaust residues such as oil and carbon particles do not travel far from the road and will be no problem unless you pick your plants very close to the traffic. It is usually perfectly obvious whether a plant is growing in acceptably clean conditions so just use your common sense.

The countryside too has its pitfalls. Roadside pollution can still be a menace, though usually less so than in town. Problems from agricultural sprays are a rare concern but you should still be careful when picking from the edge of crop fields. Cars on the move can be a nuisance and I often find myself squeezing into a prickly hedge when two cars perversely choose that particular spot to pass one another. Probably the worst problem, though not dangerous unless you happen to be in the hedge at the time, is hedge-trimming. This operation is essential – left untrimmed, hedges would cease to be hedges and attempt to join the other side of the road to make a long wood. Despite efforts by councils and farmers to cut at the right time of year (usually to accommodate nesting birds), they often seem to do so at the wrong time for the forager. Promising Redcurrant bushes, Gooseberry bushes and Hazel trees are devastated in seconds by the voracious blades of these vertical lawn mowers. In any new world order, I will have the whole process placed under my personal control. Nevertheless, we can often be lucky and find a crop that has managed to escape. My favourite hedgerow harvest – the relatively tall Elderflower – normally evades the hedge-trimmers.

Woodland edges are seldom trimmed and will often contain many edible species. The modern version of the planted hedgerow is the swathes of trees and shrubs planted by imaginative council and highway authorities along dual carriageways and even on roundabouts. My best spot for Wild Cherries is on a bypass (I won't tell you which) and the largest patch of Sea Buckthorn I have ever come across is alongside the A1 just south of Newcastle. Sometimes these places are accessible, but often they are a forage too far.

The heart of a wood is surprisingly poor foraging territory; it is generally too dark and fails to provide the 'edge habitat' required by so many plants. Wood Sorrel and Sweet Chestnut are the most likely woodland finds. Heath and bog bring Bilberry and Cranberry respectively, while streams will supply two of my favourite edible plants – Watercress and Watermint. Fields and meadows are also excellent hunting grounds with Pignut, Sorrel, Wintercress and Dandelion.

I have included a few of the plants that can be found at the seaside though you'll find them explored more thoroughly in my *Edible Seashore* handbook. I repeat them here either because they are particularly tasty or because they also occur inland.

How to look

Foraging for plants requires very little in the way of equipment, but a certain amount of preparation will make it a great deal easier – and safer. I have waded out into a chalk stream to pick Watercress in bare feet on several occasions, having forgotten my wellies. You *can* do it, but it is not fun – the water temperature feels about zero even in July. Feet are not the only parts endangered – with so many berry trees armed with spines and thorns, thick gloves and robust clothing are often an absolute necessity. I also highly recommend a hat as this will shade your eyes, protect your head, keep you dry, and double as an emergency foraging basket.

A collection of real baskets, buckets, small pots with lids and canvas bags will bring your finds home intact and, if you take enough, not hopelessly mixed together. A knife is an important part of the forager's kit, but there is now a serious obstacle to this innocent necessity. Carrying a knife in a public place with a blade longer than 75mm, or any knife with a fixed blade or a blade that can be locked in position (many penknives are like this), is a criminal offence with up to four years available to catch up on your reading. It is, however, fine if you have 'lawful excuse' – a carpenter on his way to a site job or a fisherman off to the seaside would have a good reason to carry a fixed blade, but the wild food hunter may have a harder time convincing a suspicious member of the constabulary of his innocent intentions. Of course, if you popped into the bank while on your way to your favourite Wild Garlic spot with a bowie knife tucked down your trousers you would be asking for trouble. Scissors are indispensable and I never go anywhere without a pair, even to the bank, but even these could conceivably be misconstrued as a fixed blade. A spade will be necessary for unearthing Horseradish and other roots, though how you are going to explain one of those I do not know.

Berry-pickers are the love-child of a comb and a dustpan. They can speed up the picking of Bilberries, though, by the time you have removed all the twigs and leaves in your collection, not as much as you might hope. You can either spend a day and

Forager's kit: boxwood berry-picker, knife, scissors, drainpipe picker and stick with crooked end

a half handcrafting one in finest boxwood like I did, or buy a perfectly serviceable plastic and wire one from a specialist supplier for under a tenner. Much more useful, though this time you *will* have to make it yourself, is a plum/apple/hazelnut/cherry picker fashioned from a 40mm plastic waste pipe. The fruit rolls magically down the tube into your hand or even into a bag secured at the bottom. The prongs are made by cutting and shaping the pipe into a fork, then carefully bending them by warming the plastic over a gas flame. The last bit is fraught with danger but if you keep the pipe at least 15cm above the flame you shouldn't burn yourself too badly.

A sturdy stick with a crooked end for pulling fruit- and nut-bearing branches within your grasp – and for waving at rival foragers in a threatening manner – is de rigueur.

There is one potential hazard in using these implements, or at least carrying them around in a public place – the innocent forager may be open to the accusation of 'going equipped'. Such a situation might arise, for example, if you walked past a cherry orchard on your way to pick some hedgerow plums while carrying your trusty drainpipe picker over your shoulder. This sounds, and is, ridiculous, but the penalty is up to three years inside and the police and courts do not always pursue the path of good sense.

Finally, a little-used hedgerow foraging technique that is my gift to you is the 'standing on the roof of your car' method. This is seriously effective – I once picked many kilos of plums from a tree whose lower branches had been stripped bare by less adventurous collectors. A proud moment.

When to look

Wild food can be found at any time of the year – even January – but the warmer months are always best. Spring will bring succulent new growth and Hawthorn blossoms, and summer has its Strawberries and Redcurrants, but if I were to choose the best time of all, it would be early September. Many summer fruits are still around and the autumn ones just beginning, roots are plump and green vegetables such as Watercress and Fat Hen still in leaf.

For each species I have indicated when they are most likely to appear. This is summarised in the Forager's Calendar (pp.16–19). The dates given are inevitably approximate as they can vary by a few weeks with the weather, which in turn will be influenced by geographical location. 'May' blossom from the Hawthorn, for example, is so called because of the time of its appearance, but it can often be found in June.

Forager's calendar

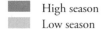 High season
Low season

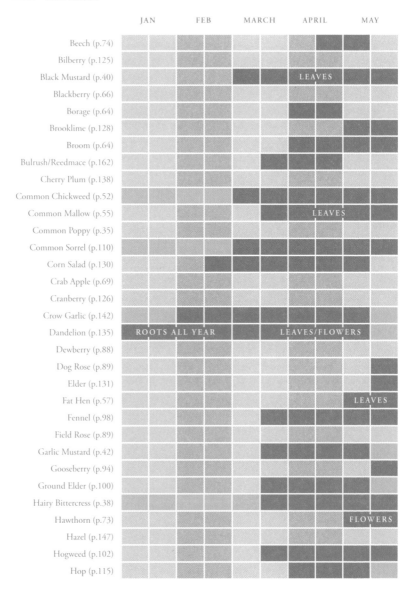

Seasons vary greatly from year to year so this is a rough and ready guide to the best times to look. Some plants have more than one crop and this is noted on the chart. The low season (shaded pale green) is when a plant may sometimes be found but is not necessarily at its best or so easy to find.

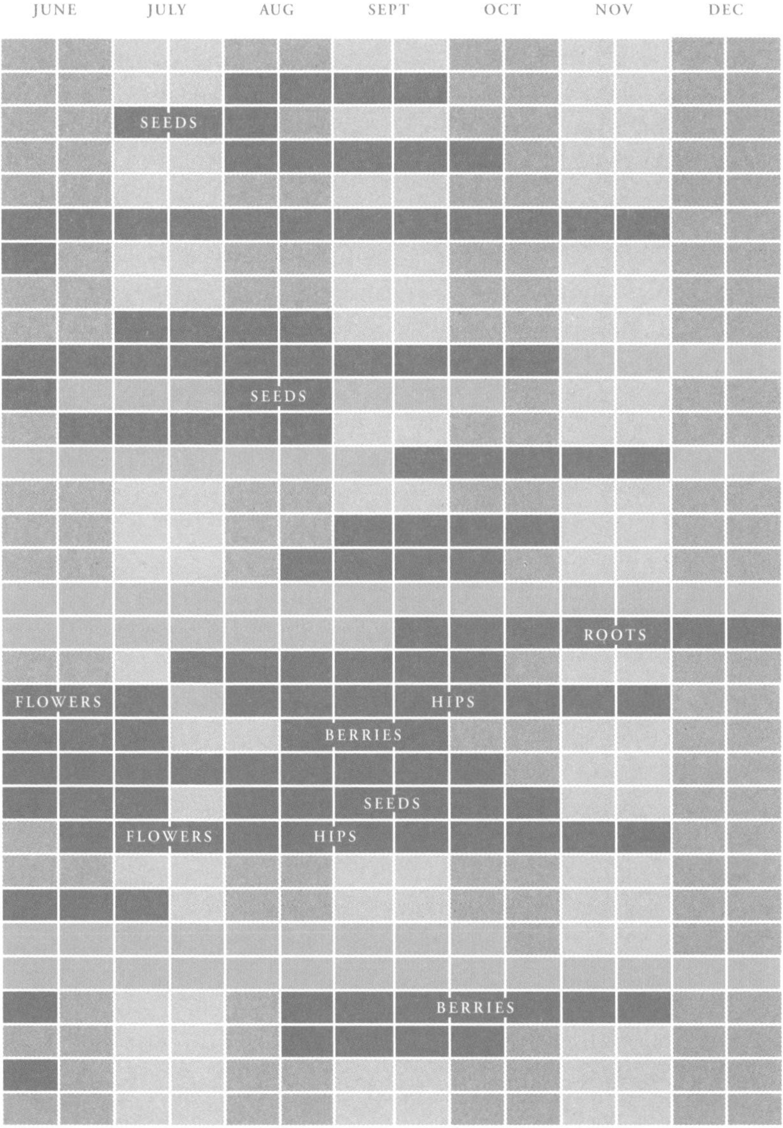
JUNE
JULY
AUG
SEPT
OCT
NOV
DEC
SEEDS
SEEDS
ROOTS
FLOWERS
HIPS
BERRIES
SEEDS
FLOWERS
HIPS
BERRIES

	JAN	FEB	MARCH	APRIL	MAY
Horseradish (p.44)					
Japanese Rose (p.91)					
Juniper (p.153)					
Lime (p.74)					
Perennial Wall Rocket (p.50)					
Pignut (p.104)					
Raspberry (p.87)					
Redcurrant (p.97)				FLOWERS	
Red Goosefoot (p.59)					
Round-leaved Mint (p.120)					
Rowan (p.75)					
Sea Buckthorn (p.156)					
Sheep's Sorrel (p.111)					
Silver Birch (p.159)					
Silverweed (p.78)					
Sloe/Blackthorn (p.81)					
Spearmint (p.120)					
Spear-leaved Orache (p.60)					
Stinging Nettle (p.112)					
Sweet Chestnut (p.151)					
Sweet Cicely (p.107)				LEAVES	
Watercress (p.47)					
Watermint (p.117)					
Wild Carrot (p.108)					
Wild Cherry (p.83)					
Wild Garlic (p.144)					
Wild Marjoram (p.123)					
Wild Parsnip (p.108)					
Wild Plum (p.138)					
Wild Strawberry (p.92)					
Wintercress (p.36)					
Wood Sorrel (p.62)					
Yarrow (p.141)					

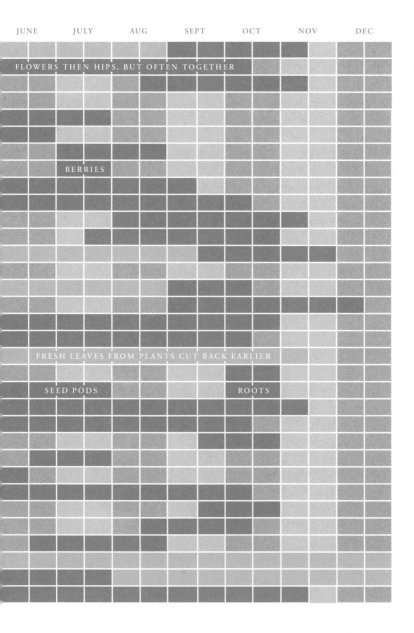

FLOWERS THEN HIPS, BUT OFTEN TOGETHER

BERRIES

FRESH LEAVES FROM PLANTS CUT BACK EARLIER

SEED PODS   ROOTS

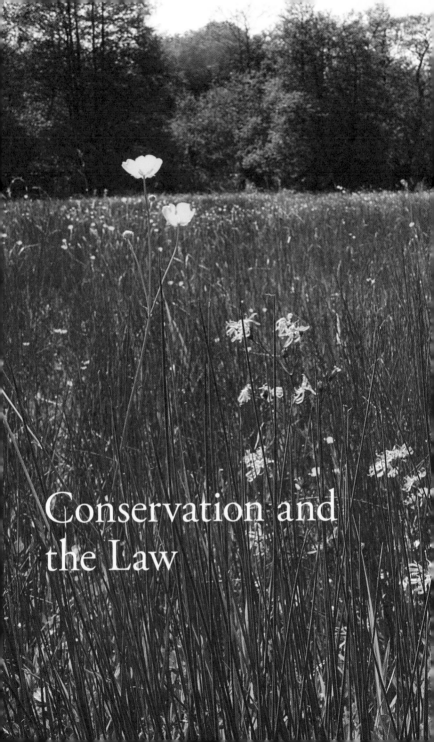

Conservation and
the Law

People can become very disquieted over the matter of conservation and foraging. Surely, they argue, we should not be taking things from the wild for our own purposes; surely nature has been injured by us enough without this further imposition. This is not an argument with which I have a great deal of sympathy. It is, of course, perfectly possible to forage in a manner that is damaging to the natural world, but it is not actually all that easy.

Many of our native species *are* under threat but it is not from the forager. Invasive species take a toll of habitats by usurping ecological niches; Japanese knotweed and Himalayan balsam being among the worst hedgerow offenders here. But most damage is done by human-induced loss of habitat. The ploughing of meadow and downland, uprooting of hedges, felling of mature woodlands, urbanisation, golf courses, industrial development or even something as simple as walking on a pebble beach (one of the problems faced by sea kale) all have a major effect on biodiversity. Habitat is everything – if the correct habitat exists, so will the species that thrive in it, foraged or not.

The commercial collection of plants has the potential to cause problems because of its likely scale, but there are few records of this actually happening. The reason for this is not hard to see. Some shellfish and some fungi are well worth the effort of gathering for reward, but it is much harder to make a living from wild plants – a kilogram of Wood Sorrel may command a high price but it will take several hours to collect.

But what if *everybody* picked wild plants? There are two ripostes to this. First of all, not everybody will. I recall watching a popular television programme where one of my favourite edible plants – Sea Beet – was enthusiastically recommended to the viewers. I worried that families would set off with baskets, boxes and large appetites on weekend trips to collect every last plant. The following season, in the half-dozen highly accessible places where I pick it myself, I could find not the slightest evidence that anyone had picked a single leaf. If anything, I rather hope that my powers of persuasion are greater than those of that television presenter. Secondly, for most of the plants in this book, it would make very little difference if everybody *did* pick them. Dandelions, Sorrel, Blackberries, Elderflowers, Sloes, Nettles, Crab Apples, Fat Hen, Hawthorn, Sweet Cicely, Sweet Chestnut, Wild Garlic, Wood Sorrel and more are so hugely abundant that it would effectively be beyond our abilities to damage them by collecting.

Remember also that when one is picking fruits the plants themselves are completely unaffected. Fruit are created, of course, in order that the plant may reproduce and not so that we might feed ourselves; it could, therefore, be argued that picking fruit might damage the long-term reproductive success of a species. This is clear nonsense because of the vast numbers of fruit (or seed) that a plant produces in its lifetime, out of which only one or two need to develop into new

Southern Marsh Orchid, *Dactylorhiza praetermissa*

mature plants. For example, how many Crab Apples would you have to gather before populations of Crab Apple trees started to decline? Well, nearly all of them, and for several decades.

There is also the plea that we should always leave some wild fruit to feed the birds. Now I like birds as much as the next man (woodcock and teal are particular favourites) and I think that if they can get to the berries before I do then jolly good luck to them.

I suspect that at least some of the concerns expressed by individuals and organisations over foraging and wildlife are not about conservation but protecting their patch – good old-fashioned territoriality. Certainly one or two of the nature wardens with whom I have 'had words' over the years, even when I was carrying no more than a camera and tripod, seemed more interested in 'seeing me off' than in seriously protecting the species on their site. Fortunately, organisations such as Plantlife and the National Trust are now, with publications and courses, actively encouraging the idea of careful foraging as a way of helping people feel that the natural world actually has something to do with them.

One sin occasionally committed by the conservation-minded is that of 'environmental colonialism' – refusing to buy or gather local wild food while cheerfully buying the imported article. A typical example of this is when a restaurant is banned, or at least discouraged, from using locally collected ceps and chanterelles on conservation grounds with no concern expressed about their being imported from who knows where. I once observed the same mindset at play in a national nature reserve where all the gates were made from tropical hardwoods.

When one considers the ethics of a particular position, they must be weighed against those of its alternative – one cannot assume that cultivated food has no negative environmental impact. Whatever food you eat, it must have come from *somewhere* and eating from the wild is, in principle at least, *more* virtuous than eating cultivated food. There are a handful of food crops which may be considered positive or at least neutral in their environmental effects – hill-grazed sheep, oysters and seaweeds being the only three I can easily bring to mind – but most are inevitably negative. Any crop – rice, wheat, potatoes, vines, olives, apples – requires that whatever wild organisms were there originally must be destroyed and then kept at bay, and we must remember that most husbanded animals are fed on crops of some sort or another.

A truly committed environmentalist who also eschewed foraging (and hunting) would probably starve to death. Foraging, by contrast, is a thoroughly virtuous exercise. If one forages from the wild, it is *still wild* afterwards and, far from being a dangerous aberration, foraging (and hunting) are the *only* natural means by which we can obtain sustenance – all others being a matter of artifice. My concern is not that we forage too much, but too little. It is admittedly a human-centred view, but there are vast quantities of wild food in our hedgerows, woods and fields and most of it goes to waste. More food taken from the wild would, in theory at least, mean that some land could be released from agriculture and reserved for wildlife.

I hope that my arguments have convinced you that foraging is not only harmless but positively beneficial. But, of course, with a bit of effort, it is still perfectly possible to turn yourself into a walking ecological disaster. For example, picking Blackberries is clearly a benign activity, but trampling over lady slipper orchids to do it is not. Always tread carefully where there might be delicate organisms that could be damaged. This applies particularly to things like Marsh Samphire, Watercress and Watermint, which are found in sensitive habitats.

Here is a brief, and rather obvious, guide on how to get it right:

1. Take care not to damage habitats by trampling all over them.
2. Most of the plants in this book are very common but one or two are not and should be picked with extreme care and only occasionally. I have indicated the conservation status of most of the species I describe.
3. Obey the laws that cover conservation.
4. Although it hardly applies to such things as Blackberries and Haws, in general it is wise to pick a little here and a little there of whatever you are collecting. A woodland floor stripped of its Wood Sorrel, for example, is a forlorn sight.

You may now enjoy your foraging in the certain knowledge of your virtue.

The law

The law of foraging has never been an entirely settled matter and many pitfalls exist to catch out the unwary forager. There are three legal areas to consider – access, ownership and conservation. If you cannot bear to plough through this section, and who can blame you, there's a more digestible summary at the end.

First things first. If you venture on to private land for whatever purpose, without explicit or implicit permission from the owner, then you are trespassing. (Note that there is no law of trespass in Scotland, where there is an admirable and long-established right to roam almost everywhere.) If you do stray on to private land without permission then you will not be committing a crime. It will be, rather, a civil wrong so you cannot be prosecuted, no matter what the signs say. You could, however, be sued, even if you do not damage anything or make a thorough nuisance of yourself – the landowner could sue for the hypothetical advantage you receive from being on his or her land. If asked to leave, you must do so by the nearest exit. There are many places where implicit permission may be given – land owned by the Forestry Commission, National Trust and local authority land, Wildlife Trust nature reserves and so on.

The fundamental law governing foraging is the common law right to collect the 'four 'f's – fruit, flowers, fungi and foliage'. This applies with two provisos – first that the material picked is for personal use, not commercial gain, and second that it is growing wild. You could, for example, pick five kilos of Crab Apples from a farmer's hedge but could not sell the jelly you made from it at the local bring-and-buy sale. You could *not* pick five kilos of apples from an orchard – that would be stealing. Similarly if the Crab Apples had been purposely planted as a crop then again that would count as theft.

This principle is helpfully enshrined in the 1968 Theft Act which states that '*A person who picks mushrooms growing wild on any land, or who picks flowers, fruit or foliage from a plant growing wild on any land, does not (although not in possession of the land) steal what he picks, unless he does it for reward or for sale or other commercial purpose. (For purposes of this subsection 'mushroom' includes any fungus, and 'plant' includes any shrub or tree.)*'

Note that the act refers twice to '*any land* ', and uses the phrase '*although not in possession of the land* ', meaning that even if someone is trespassing they will not be stealing. The picking would merely constitute a further act of trespass and this is not a matter for the criminal law. One interesting practical consideration here is that if a landowner caught you with a basket of those Crab Apples picked from a wild tree growing on his land he could not demand them from you, though explaining this to him would likely tax your debating skills. His only redress would be to sue for the value of the apples.

The main message from this, however, is that gathering wild food in a place to which you are permitted access is legal and can be done without having to look over your shoulder. There are, inevitably, exceptions. On some land this right has been withdrawn with a byelaw forbidding the collection of any plant, fungus or animal. There should be a sign to this effect somewhere near the entrance. It is possible to challenge these byelaws if you feel really strongly about them (and you have money lying around the house in drifts) and this has been done successfully in the past, such as at Strangford Lough, N.I., where a winkle picker successfully contested a National Trust byelaw banning the collection of shellfish.

A second, and even more irritating, exception is on land made newly accessible under the Countryside and Rights of Way Act 2000 (CROW). This generally welcome act has made large tracts of land legally accessible to walkers, but confers no right to collect wild food (or anything else) that exists there. The act states that a person is not entitled to be on the land if he '*… intentionally removes, damages or destroys any plant, shrub, tree or root, or any part of a plant, shrub, tree or root.*' Fortunately this does not remove existing rights of foraging in places such as where

a footpath passes over land now within the act or any common land which the act may encompass. The wording of the act makes the picking of, say, Blackberries on land where access was not previously allowed an act of trespass (not, it must be stressed, theft) and the law requires that a person doing such a thing remove themselves immediately for a period of 72 hours, presumably to give them a chance to reconsider their lives.

There is, in fact, almost nothing you can do on CROW land other than walk across it. It is, for example, technically against the provisions of the act to go on to such land if you have head lice as the only animal you are allowed to take with you is a dog; you are also not allowed to annoy people or engage in a Scrabble tournament (no organised games). While you are sat there, peacefully not scratching your head or playing Scrabble, you can at least enjoy a picnic which *is* allowed. I have read quite a few acts of Parliament over the years while studying the law as it pertains to foraging and have concluded that they are largely drawn up by lunatics.

Conservation law is an added burden. The popular works of Beatrice Potter seem to be the main authority for much of this legislation, not scientific studies or common sense. It is the bluntness of the laws that cause the problems, not their good intentions. The 1981 Wildlife and Countryside Act states that: '... *if any person... not being an authorised person, intentionally uproots any wild plant... he shall be guilty of an offence.*'

This seems like a perfectly reasonable law until one tries to imagine the problem it was intended to solve. It does not, of itself, prevent a farmer from ploughing up a field containing plants, rare or otherwise, as the farmer would be an authorised person. Foragers, on the other hand, have never been a threat to wildlife when collecting Dandelion or burdock roots. Apart from the casual or commercial (and remember, commercial collecting is already an offence) uprooting of bluebell and snowdrop bulbs and maybe the odd collector of rare plants digging up a lizard orchid, there never was a problem to solve. Now the roots of common plants are out of bounds and the absurd situation exists where an annual plant can be cut off at just above ground level, effectively killing it, but pulling it up by the roots is a criminal offence – Hairy Bittercress and Marsh Samphire are two plants to which this applies. The answer, such as it is, is to become an authorised person and obtain permission from the land owner.

Certain plants mentioned in the 1981 act are on the famous 'schedule 8' list and it is illegal to damage them in any way. None of these rare plants are recommended in this book.

Some of the best foraging sites are, inevitably, on Sites of Special Scientific Interest (SSSIs). There are approaching 10,000 of these in Britain. Many are on private land with no public access, but some are open to the public. There are a couple of problems for the forager under the terms of the 1981 act which establishes these sites. When a site is registered as an SSSI, a list is drawn up of species which made it interesting in the first place and it is illegal to damage any of these organisms. This is unlikely to affect most foraging excursions, but a few plants in this book are sufficiently special to warrant a mention in the declaration of an SSSI – Cranberry and Juniper are two which come to mind.

More serious is something else that is published with the declaration of a site – an ominous list of 'operations likely to damage' the SSSI. These activities are not necessarily banned, but consultation with, and permission from Natural England, the government agency that administers the act, would be required before they could take place. A list will often include such obvious things as quarrying and tree-felling, but there is also a catch-all along the lines of 'removal of or damage to any plant, fungus or animal'. Natural England and the other conservation authorities are, however, generally sensible bodies, which understand that picking Blackberries, Sloes or Sorrel is not going to do any harm at all and are unlikely to seek prosecution for the restrained collection of such common plants.

If you manage to negotiate these arcane rules and miss out on your fun day in court there is one further (and potentially more serious) pitfall awaiting the unwary forager – the law which deals with the carrying of knives and other foraging equipment. See Starting Out (pp.13–15) for the hair-raising details.

Good luck. I hope you don't need it.

Here is that summary:

1. You need permission to go on to land you do not own, otherwise you will be trespassing. This does not apply in Scotland.
2. There is a common law right, enshrined in law, that you may collect 'fruit, flowers, fungi and foliage', providing it is for personal use only and is growing wild.
3. Byelaws exist in some places which have removed these rights.
4. This right does not exist on CROW land unless it existed before the land was registered under the act.
5. It is illegal to uproot any plant without permission from the owner of the land on which it grows.
6. Some (rare) plants are protected by law.
7. Plants cited in the declaration of an SSSI are protected.
8. Picking any plants on an SSSI may, strictly, be illegal but it is unlikely that picking common plants such as Blackberries and Sorrel will result in prosecution.

Edible Species

The seventy or so species described here are the best wild food plants that the British Isles have to offer. It is not a comprehensive list – there are many more edible plants than this, but most are uncommon or just don't taste all that great. I have chosen those you are most likely to find and most likely to enjoy. There are a few omissions which may seem odd to the seasoned forager. For example, I have left out bistort and tansy because I don't think they taste very nice, and Comfrey because it is seriously poisonous if eaten in large quantities. There are also a few oddities which I've included because they are interesting for some reason or other – Yarrow and Brooklime being two such. For a more complete list I highly recommend Richard Mabey's justly famous *Food for Free*.

If you are new to foraging I suspect the one thing that will surprise you is not necessarily the number of species that can be found, but just how much of many of them can be easily (and sustainably) collected. A small, expensive packet of supermarket salad looks quite pitiful next to a basketful of Wild Rocket that has been gathered for nothing in a few minutes. And a punnet containing half a dozen under-ripe cultivated plums looks rather dismal compared to a car boot full of glorious, and free, wild Cherry Plums.

I know that many people are concerned that a walk on the wild side will quickly see them in hospital. But although there are plants that will kill you before you can get to the nearest A&E, the sensible forager need not worry. Most edible plants are distinctive enough (everyone knows what a Stinging Nettle, Hazelnut and Raspberry look like) and if you are not sure whether you can tell a Red Goosefoot from a Black Nightshade then you should just not bother with it. I have eaten around one hundred species of wild plant and one hundred and thirty species of wild fungi and have never – well, not yet – had as much as a mild stomach ache. It is just a matter of being extremely careful and, above all, not jumping to conclusions. Remember, accidentally killing yourself by eating a poisonous plant for your tea may be a painful tragedy for you and your nearest, but, worse still, it is so *embarrassing*.

The good news is that identification is much, much easier in the plant world than it is in the fungal world, where there is little obvious difference between an edible Blusher and a poisonous Panther Cap – like most mushrooms and toadstools they both have a cap and a stem and accurate identification is all down to the fine details. With plants, however, there are enormous differences in general size, leaf shape, flower structure, growth habit and so on. Still, you will need to proceed carefully with some species, observing each characteristic in turn.

Most plants in this book present no problem – few people will confuse a Blackberry, Raspberry, Crab Apple or even Fennel with anything else. Nevertheless, identification is not always straightforward. Since we are often interested in just the young leaves, we may not always have the most useful identifying feature, the flower, to help us.

While there are endless ways of getting things wrong, there are three areas of particular concern: berries, the potato family and the carrot family. Many berries are good to eat but some equally tasty-looking ones can be seriously poisonous. Fortunately, most are quite distinctive and you will have the added assistance of leaves and growth habit to make you certain of your identification. Plants are put into families for the simple reason that they are related to one another. This also means that, like all families, they share certain characteristics.

There are two seriously treacherous families in this book, the carrot family and the potato family. Both contain plants that are very good to eat, but also plants that will have you in A&E – if you are lucky enough to get there in time. No wild member of the potato family in this country is edible, but some species do have leaves which can look superficially like those of some edible plants, particularly the goosefoots. The carrot family does include native edible species; the issue here is distinguishing between these and the poisonous carrots, most notably Hemlock Water-dropwort. I have tried to warn of these possible confusions so that when, say, you pick Fat Hen, you will be quite sure that you have not picked Black Nightshade by mistake.

I have avoided technical terms as much as possible – too much, my botanist friends might say – as most people will throw their hands up in despair when presented with phrases such as '*lvs oblong, sinuate-dentate to pinnatifid, lower narrowed into the stalk, the upper sessile or amplexicaul*', and I decided that general clarity was preferable to academic precision.

A mistake I see again and again is people making up their mind about something and ignoring clear features that indicate that it cannot possibly be what they think it is. A typical example would be, 'I am sure it is Fat Hen though the leaves are a bit hairy.' Fat Hen *never* has hairy leaves so it *must* be something else. Another mistake is to flick through a book to find something that 'looks a bit like it'. There is nothing wrong with flicking through books, we all do it, but it is essential to double check that all the characters you are expecting are actually there.

This handbook alone should suffice when it comes to identifying the various wild foods, but there is nothing wrong with double checking in a wild-flower field guide. Not that I recommend you join me in Anorak World with fifteen books to plough through. The internet is also a good place to find pictures of plants, but it can be unreliable. To use our example above, an image search for Fat Hen may well present you with a picture of Black Nightshade instead because it just happens to be on the same web page as Fat Hen as a comparison – so do be careful.

Eventually you will be able to spot a member of the goosefoot family from ten paces and provide its Latin name at five – it is all a matter of practice.

Common Poppy *Papaver rhoeas*

DESCRIPTION	Medium annual, to 90cm. Leaves deeply divided, with pointed irregular lobes, hairy. Stem hairy. Flowers scarlet, often a small dark patch at base of petals, many successive flowers on one plant. Seeds in lidded cups
HABITAT	Cornfields, disturbed ground
DISTRIBUTION	Very common in England, except the Northwest. Scarce in central Wales, Northern Ireland and in Scotland, except the Southeast
SEASON	Seed heads mature from late June until August

Nothing is more evocative of high summer than an inadvertent field of Poppies. These are less frequent today, but sometimes a corner or a strip of field escapes the herbicidal sprays and the dormant Common Poppy takes its chance to turn it scarlet. The ephemeral flower is the colour of fresh blood and a reminder of the Western Front where so many lost their lives; the plant germinates in disturbed soil and none were so disturbed as those of Belgium and France during the First World War.

Apart from fields, the Common Poppy is common everywhere from gardens to grassy banks. All parts are poisonous except the seeds and it is these that we eat. Timing is everything as the seed heads should be picked just as they ripen and open – before this the seeds are not ready; after and the seed heads will likely be empty. Pull the seed heads off and place them in a bag or plastic box – a basket is obviously not suitable as the seeds will fall through.

If necessary leave them a few days to ripen and when the heads rattle with their seeds turn them upside down and shake, or, to speed things up, prise the lids off first. The nutty flavour of the seeds is very familiar baked on bread and there really is no better way of using them, although they are also used to flavour cakes.

Also look out for the Opium Poppy (*P. somniferum*).

The seeds of the Common Poppy and all our other native poppies are tiny and you will need to find a large number of seed heads for a worthwhile collection. Much more rewarding are the seed heads of the Opium Poppy, which are comparatively huge and full of large seeds. These seeds can be used, as above, in bread- and cake-making. The Opium Poppy has almost the same distribution as the Common Poppy but with a preference for the seaside in the North. Roadsides and gardens are typical habitats for this flamboyant and distinctive plant. With its broad blue/green leaves and large pink flowers it is unmistakable.

Wintercresses *Barbarea* spp.

DESCRIPTION	Medium/tall perennial, 40–80cm. Upright from basal rosette of leaves. Leaves with deep leaflet-like lobes, in several pairs. Hairless. Flowers four-petalled, yellow
HABITAT	Hedges, stream banks, damp ploughed fields
DISTRIBUTION	Common Wintercress: very common in England, rare in the west of Scotland and central-west Wales. Fairly common in Northern Ireland. American Wintercress: occasional in southern and western England, coastal in Wales, scarce elsewhere
SEASON	All year, but best in winter and early spring

It is a pleasure to see the rosettes of dark, shiny green leaves of Wintercress amidst the barren landscape of January. Common Wintercress (*B. vulgaris*) is the most common of the four species of *Barbarea* in the British Isles, followed by the very similar but alien American Wintercress (*B. verna)*, which actually originated in southwest Europe – it is just popular in America. Both these provide a winter salad from their basal leaves when almost nothing else is growing. Not that everyone will be pleased to see it on their plate – the leaves are peppery and quite bitter and perhaps unsuitable for the effete modern palate. In 1847 a gardening manual dismissed both plants, saying they were '*subordinate to the Watercress in every character, and our pages may be occupied with more useful subjects*'.

The only thing to do, of course, is find some and try it. The place where the photograph (opposite) was taken is a typical habitat – a damp field edge. Sadly this was the only plant intact – the others had been nibbled by roe deer, judging by nearby signs (you know you have lived in the country too long when you can identify animals by their poo). In fact any damp but not boggy area is likely to be a good hunting ground.

The two species are difficult to tell apart when young (not that it matters very much, except that American Wintercress is a little milder). If you want to know the difference, the Common Wintercress has only two or three pairs of lobes to the American Wintercress's half-dozen. In the mature plant the former has unlobed side leaves and shorter seed pods.

The leaves can be cooked, though this seems to enhance rather than diminish the bitterness. The best thing is to use them in a salad with some other milder-flavoured leaf. A first-class oil and some cider vinegar will help.

American Winterress

Hairy Bittercress *Cardamine hirsuta*

DESCRIPTION	Small annual. Leaves form a small rosette about 10cm across. Leaves sparsely hairy, opposite, with one terminal leaflet. Flowers tiny, white, four-petalled. Seed pods slender, upright and explosive!
HABITAT	Waste ground, gardens, walls, field edges, path edges
DISTRIBUTION	Extremely common throughout the British Isles, though rare in the Scottish Highlands
SEASON	All year

Most of the weeds sent to build the characters of gardeners are tenacious perennials such as bindweed and Ground Elder, but one annual – Hairy Bittercress – is a match for them all. This uncommonly short-lived little plant will appear suddenly in any neglected corner of the garden and has a particular liking for flower tubs. A single plant can, from germination to explosive dissemination, produce five hundred seeds in a couple of months and an unweeded flower bed can be quickly overrun. Hoed, sprayed or uprooted, it is almost invariably discarded as the pernicious weed it certainly is, but this is a sad waste. Neither particularly hairy nor bitter the 'cress' part of its name, at least, is appropriate, for the flavour is indistinguishable from that of the familiar sandwich ingredient. This prosaic weed is fresh and nutty in flavour and, in my opinion, the very best of the wild salad vegetables.

Hairy Bittercress is a member of the cabbage family and has several close relatives which are all edible. If you find Bittercress in woodland it is more likely to be Wood Bittercress (*C. flexuosa*) and if it is unusually large then it is probably Large Bittercress (*C. amara*). The Reverend Johns in his *Botanical Rambles* describes Hairy Bittercress as having 'few pretensions to beauty', but there is a member of the *Cardamine* genus which needs no pretence; it is that denizen of wet meadows, the lovely Lady's Smock (*C. pratensis*). Although edible, this plant is both bitter and too pretty to pick.

Hairy Bittercress is best collected by snipping off the leaves with scissors although I often uproot entire plants (legal niceties being more than usually absurd in this instance), then trim away the root to avoid getting dirt everywhere. Some of the best plants are found growing at the edges of pavements but these tend to suffer much in the way of pollution, particularly that of a canine nature.

There is really nothing dangerous with which the various Bittercresses might be confused, but the related Scurvygrasses look superficially similar. They have a rosette of single, heart-shaped leaves. These are edible, though only in the loosest sense of the word, being extremely bitter.

Black Mustard *Brassica nigra*

DESCRIPTION	Large annual up to 2 metres high. Large, deeply lobed, stalked leaves, very rough surface. Flowers yellow, four-petalled. Seeds black, in small erect pods. All parts taste very strongly of mustard
HABITAT	Seaside cliff edges, waste ground, river banks
DISTRIBUTION	Fairly common, local. Chiefly in England south of the Wash. Almost entirely coastal in Wales
SEASON	Leaves are at their best in spring, but can be found for much of the year in sheltered places. Seeds in July and August

This native annual has long been cultivated and is the original mustard. It is found most readily on cliff edges, explaining perhaps its neglect by the average forager. Although commonly used as a spice and salad ingredient, historically its main use has always been as a medicine. Anything with so potent a flavour as mustard is bound to attract the attention of herbalists who, sometimes rightly, assume that such a plant must have considerable power over the body. Of potential interest to the forager is its reputed ability to resist '*the malignity of mushrooms*'; however, Culpeper is not only the most entertaining herbalist, he is also the most unreliable. He also tells us that it is good for the '*falling down sickness*', the '*drowsy and forgetful evil*' and that it '*helps toothache*'. The latter has some truth in it. A mouthful of mustard tends to take your mind off your molars.

Three crops can be obtained from Black Mustard – the leaves, the young flower heads and the seeds. Seen in a greengrocer's, the leaves would most likely be passed over by most customers. They are fairly tough and have the surface texture of a scouring pad. None of this really matters; the flavour is worth it. I well remember my first taste, many years ago. There was a certain amount of running around and a lot of gasping. It was the surprise as much as the heat.

Black Mustard is great in a beef sandwich as a pleasant cross between horseradish and a green salad. The hot mustard taste of the raw leaves only appears after a bit of chewing. For this reason a pesto is the best way of using it – the mastication has effectively been done for you.

The bright yellow/green young flower heads are succulent and spicy, if a little bitter. Steam them for just a few minutes and serve with butter, or you could use them in the pesto. Don't pick every one you can find, however, as you will then miss out on Black Mustard's third crop – the seeds.

These are the hottest of all the mustards; English mustard is a blend of Black and the milder White Mustard, together with some flour and turmeric. As Black Mustard seeds are tiny and form in short pods, they are very difficult to collect. Timing is difficult too – I arrived a week late at one of my Black Mustard spots and could find barely a half-teaspoonful – the rest had been scattered. The surest way is to cut the flower spikes while the pods are slightly under-ripe, then thresh out the seeds on to a sheet when ready.

Garlic Mustard *Alliaria petiolata*

DESCRIPTION	Erect biennial, usually single-stemmed, 1 metre tall. Leaves bright, light green, hairless; heart-shaped, more pointedly so with upper leaves, more rounded with the lower leaves; bluntly toothed edge. Flowers four-petalled, white. Smells of garlic when crushed
HABITAT	Shady hedgerows, woodland edges
DISTRIBUTION	Very common throughout the British Isles, except in north and west Scotland and in Northern Ireland
SEASON	March–May, although new leaves can appear in the autumn

This cheerful-looking spring cabbage seems to harbour an odd desire to become a garlic plant. Untouched, the leaves are odourless, but when crushed or chewed the garlic aroma becomes immediately apparent. In addition to the name given here it is also commonly known as Hedge Garlic, Jack-in-the-hedge and, in the past, Sauce-alone – the latter being a reference either to its comprehensive talents as a flavouring or an unlikely corruption of *Sauce-ail* where *ail* is the French for 'garlic'.

As few shady hedgerows will fail to support a colony or two of this stately herb and it is a very easy plant to identify, Garlic Mustard is a reliable hedgerow favourite. Although it is familiar as a tall and erect plant, the rounded kidney-shaped basal leaves can be found from early in the year. The best time to pick it, however, is just as the flowers start to appear – much later and the flavour becomes rather rank. The small, bright leaves towards the top of the plant are the best. The roots, too, taste powerfully of garlic but they are rather thin.

Not everyone appreciates Garlic Mustard's virtues. In North America its introduction as a herb has been a small ecological disaster as, having no natural enemies there, it has displaced many native plants. The nineteenth-century writer Anne Manning described it thus: '*as ugly a Jack as one need wish to see, breathing odiously of garlic*'. For most people the flavour will be a pleasant mixture of mild garlic and mild mustard. It is most often employed as a salad vegetable or in a sauce to go with lamb. However, there is no reason why it should not be cooked; it is, after all, a type of cabbage. Serving it as a boiled vegetable is not a rewarding activity, but crispy Garlic Mustard, where the leaves are rolled up, shredded and deep-fried gives an interesting wild equivalent of the crispy 'seaweed' sold in Chinese restaurants. Perhaps most sensible is to employ it as a filling in Hen Chicken (p.215), instead of Fat Hen. Of course you will ruin the pun if you do.

P.S. Despite the unsurprising fact that Garlic Mustard tastes of garlic and mustard there are no garlic or mustard flavours in the plant – technically it is almost tasteless. When the leaves are bruised or chewed, however, chemical precursors are transformed, through a series of complex reactions, into these flavours. The mustard component is allyl isothiocyanate and the garlic flavour diallyl disulphide (the same as in true garlic). Mustard and garlic are not, generally speaking, welcome flavours for most animals and it is for this reason that the plant creates them. It is, however, a strategy that seriously backfired when it encountered the catholic palate of *Homo sapiens*.

Horseradish *Armoracia rusticana*

DESCRIPTION	Medium, leafy perennial, to 70cm, or 1.2 metres when flowering. Leaves in upright clusters, highly distinctive, large, broad, crinkling, 'fish-bone'-like pattern of veins, bright, fresh green. Flowers four-petalled, white – but flowers irregularly in the British Isles
HABITAT	Waste ground, roadsides, field edges
DISTRIBUTION	Very common in England though less so in the North, and coastal in the far Southwest. Coastal in Wales. Rare in Scotland and Northern Ireland
SEASON	All year, but best in the autumn (after this the leaves are gone and you can't find them!)

I distinctly remember trying some of my father's Horseradish Sauce when I was just nine years old. I decided immediately that it was, like girls, something I would only come to appreciate later in life. Well, it took much longer to learn to love the former than the latter, and only in the last few years have I taken to having it with my beef.

Horseradish is a fairly recent addition to our landscape, having been introduced from eastern Europe in the Middle Ages. Like so many invaders it has never found a truly wild home here, being content with disturbed and peripheral land, such as roadsides. In some parts of England, Norfolk for example, it has become a dominant roadside plant, its startlingly bright-green summer foliage extending for miles.

The leaves that will lead you to the edible root are very distinctive, but confusion with superficially similar large dock leaves is not impossible. Not that such a mistake is dangerous – you just won't find any Horseradish roots. A differentiation is simple: dock leaves usually have a little bit of red about them; they are not so bright a green; they do not have the distinct 'fish-bone' vein markings; and the base of the stem does not exude a white fluid which tastes of Horseradish.

It is possible to eat Horseradish leaves, though they are pretty tasteless – like a poor and slightly bitter cabbage. But it is, of course, the roots that are eaten, and these are not at all without taste. Being roots, they will obviously have to be dug up and Horseradish collecting suffers more than any other foraging pursuit from the prohibition against uprooting plants without permission. Considering the vast swathes of the plant that go uncollected, this is a great pity, but if you want to keep within the law, permission is what you must get. The end of October and beginning of November is the best time – the roots are full and fat and, a most practical consideration, if you leave it any longer the leaves will wither and disappear and you

won't be able to find the roots at all (I know, I have tried). Seeing the leaves will also ensure that the roots you are digging up *are* Horseradish and not some other, perhaps deadly, root such as Hemlock Water-dropwort.

It is fair to say that Horseradish roots are not easy to unearth. They are branched and twisted and tend to grow in soil with more than its fair share of large stones. Once you have your prize, take it home and wash off all the soil. The roots will keep for a long time if they are stored in sand to keep out the light and stop them drying. One other possible way exists for preserving Horseradish – scrub, slice thinly across the root, dry the slices very slowly on a warm windowsill or in a low oven, then powder the dried slices in a blender.

But Horseradish ideally should be used raw and freshly grated. I have tried cooking it as a vegetable, but the spiciness turns to bitterness and the texture is that of wet kindling wood. To prepare Horseradish, peel off the thin skin with a potato peeler, then grate the root across the grain. I have never been caught in a tear-gas attack but I can't imagine it is as bad as grating Horseradish. Do it outside on a windy day. One cooked dish which does work very well is Horseradish and Chestnut Dumplings (p.216). The very light cooking the grated root receives ensures that the aromatic flavour does not turn bitter.

There are many recipes for Horseradish Sauce, each seeming to outdo the next in potency. Ignoring those that call for chilli powder, cloves or anchovies, the simplest recipe is to mix 100g grated Horseradish root with 2 tsp cider vinegar, 1 tsp ground mustard seed, 125ml double cream and a little salt and black pepper. The sauce should be kept in the fridge and used within 24 hours.

Watercress *Rorippa nasturtium-aquaticum*

DESCRIPTION	Large trailing aquatic perennial. Leaflets more or less opposite plus terminal leaflet, *very shallowly lobed* edges, dark green, often with a bronze tinge. Young leaves form a rosette around emerging flower heads. Taste *peppery*. Flowers small, white, four-petalled
HABITAT	Shallow streams, often chalk streams, ditches
DISTRIBUTION	Common, less so in the North
SEASON	Late March until November

Few wild plants come in such abundance as Watercress. It is usually possible to pick a sackful of leaves in a few minutes with little noticeable effect on the local plant population. The high price it commands in the shops makes this all the more welcome. Watercress is exactly the same delicious plant cultivated or wild – there has been no effort, or need, to improve it.

There *are* a couple of problems, however. The first comes in the form of a look-alike – Fool's Watercress (*Apium nodiflorum*). This is not nearly as bad as it sounds, for it too is edible, though much inferior, with a mild taste of carrots. It grows in precisely the same locations, often found unhelpfully intertwined with true Watercress and still gives me pause even after years of familiarity with both species. The distinguishing features of Fool's Watercress are finely and bluntly toothed edges to the leaflets, shiny yellow/green opposite leaflets and a taste of carrots.

The second problem is less easy to overcome. There is a little creature, a fluke, called *Fasciola hepatica*, which spends part of its time stuck to aquatic plants waiting to enter the digestive tract of a sheep or other herbivore. It has a baroquely complex life-cycle with about ten stages, three of which it enjoys inside a small snail. The last of these stages, the cercarium, leaves the snail and swims around until it finds a plant to attach itself to, turns into a cyst called a metacercarium and waits. The process generally requires a habitat which includes grazing animals, slow-flowing or stagnant water, muddy river banks to harbour the snails, and suitable vegetation.

F. hepatica is not a natural parasite of humans, but the tiny metacercarium will gradually develop and eat its way through you until it is at the 3cm, flat, slug-like adult stage, whereupon it finds its way into your liver. There it will be a further nuisance – blocking bile ducts, causing infections and hepatitis and eating more bits of you. As an infected person will often have many flukes sitting in their bile ducts it is sometimes, unsurprisingly, fatal. Although around two and a half million people are infected worldwide by various routes, it is difficult to quantify the problem in this

Watercress

Fool's Watercress

country where little wild Watercress is eaten. However, *F. hepatica* is very common here (millions of sheep suffer its depredations every year), so the risk is a real one.

I presume you will not be wanting a family of slug look-alikes taking up residence in your liver so my advice must be not to bother with raw wild Watercress. There is of course one simple way of removing the parasite – cooking. This would mean that salads are off the menu but there are still many excellent recipes which use cooked Watercress. But if you still want to eat it raw and wild I offer the following suggestions. Collect in fast-moving water upstream of any grazing animals. Avoid streams with muddy banks – these can harbour the snail, which acts as an unwilling accomplice to the fluke. Pick from plants that are growing in the middle of streams – you never see snails doing the breast stroke so these plants are less likely to be infected by snails climbing the stems. Choose leaves that are never submerged in water and thus out of reach of the swimming cercaria – this is easier with the large mature plants of summer. When you get home soak the collection in 10 per cent white vinegar solution for 10 minutes, then rinse very thoroughly. Alternatively, and more reliably, chlorine-based proprietary sterilisers (such as the ones used to sterilise baby's bottles) will both kill and remove the metacercaria. The latter rather detracts from the wild, natural quality of your salad but is no worse than the chlorine sterilisation of domestic water supplies.

In the eighteenth century, the writer George Saville Carey penned a slightly invigorating poem about a watercress girl, Phoebe, he met on the way to London.

> *When hoary frost hung on each thorn,*
> *Ere night had well withdrawn her gloom,*
> *Poor Phoebe went one wintry morn,*
> *From Colnbrook, down to Langley-broom,*
> *When from the brake or from the rill,*
> *Half clad and with neglected tresses,*
> *Her rushy basket try'd to fill,*
> *With fresh and green SPRING WATER CRESSES.*

There is more but I think we have had enough. I always go fully clothed and brush my hair, but the basket is a good idea. Wellies and a large pair of scissors complete the essential Watercress foraging kit. Every part of the plant is edible, but I usually collect the rosette around the developing flower head.

Assuming you successfully navigate the dreaded fluke peril, Watercress has genuine health-giving properties, as it is packed with copious quantities of vitamins, minerals and phytochemicals. The peppery taste is immediately recognisable and is common to many other members of the cabbage family. Its potency is diminished with cooking so quickly sweating it for a sauce or adding it at the very last minute to a soup is the best way to retain the flavour.

Perennial Wall Rocket

Diplotaxis tenuifolia

DESCRIPTION	Medium bush-like perennial, to 1 metre. Leaves long and irregularly lobed, tasting nutty at first then hot and peppery. Last year's stems usually visible amongst the leaves. Flowers yellow, four-petalled. Long, thin seed pods
HABITAT	Mostly coastal or urban
DISTRIBUTION	Largest population in the far southeast of England including London, but also Bristol, Liverpool and several other cities. Rare in Scotland and absent from Ireland. Scattered elsewhere, mostly coastal
SEASON	March–July

One naturally assumes that the country mouse will have the edge over the city mouse when it comes to foraging, but it is not always so. I have never seen Perennial Wall Rocket in a truly wild location, the nearest to this being a seaside car park near Weymouth, which is skirted with a couple of dozen substantial bushes. My best find of this plant ever was in the old industrial centre of Bristol where Perennial Wall Rocket grows from every crack in the concrete. It was a fairly dog-free place so I happily filled a couple of bags.

The leaves grow in little bunches all the way up the stem and you can simply cut these off. There is really nothing nasty that can be confused with Perennial Wall Rocket and the nutty, peppery flavour alone will be sufficient to reassure you. Just watch out for those dogs.

Perennial Wall Rocket is an alien invader, though a well-behaved and welcome one, and the same plant as the wild rocket one often sees in supermarkets and greengrocers. I have made polite enquiries to a couple of retail outlets, asking how they justify the 'wild' part of the name (the staff do not collect the stuff from the hedgerow on their way to work) and received charming, evasive replies in return. I guess we will never know.

The flavour of the truly wild plant is the same as that of the cultivated 'wild' plant, except that it is considerably nuttier and very considerably more peppery. If you are man enough, or indeed woman enough, there is no reason why you could not eat it alone in a salad, but I generally mix it with other milder salad leaves. Either way, I love it.

Common Chickweed *Stellaria media*

DESCRIPTION	Low, sprawling annual. Tangled habit, individual strands up to 50cm long. Leaves 1–2.5cm, oval, mostly hairless, slightly frosted. Stems straggling, *single line of hairs* down one side. Flowers five-petalled, though petals are very deeply divided and look more like ten
HABITAT	Gardens, dung heaps, field margins. Prefers damp areas
DISTRIBUTION	Very common throughout the British Isles
SEASON	Can be found all year, but only in sheltered locations during the winter. Summer growth can be stringy

Common Chickweed is not a popular plant, as anyone who has spent an hour uprooting it from their vegetable garden, only to have it defiantly reappear a couple of weeks later, will tell you. Yet as one who has forsaken the embattled life of the gardener for the lazy pursuits of the forager, it is something I am always pleased to see. Common Chickweed is one of the tastiest of the wild greens and the enlightened gardener should view it not as a threat, but as a welcome bonus crop.

The name comes from the practice of feeding it to poultry who love the stuff. Generations of budgerigars have also enjoyed this plant, and it has been used as an occasional fodder crop for cattle. Apart from its edible uses, Chickweed has found employment in a variety of dubious medical remedies. An eye lotion is one such, and its habit of closing its leaves at night has inspired its use as an inducer of sleep.

Chickweed is clearly not a hard plant to find, and its almost continual appearance throughout the year will ensure you a fairly constant supply. Avoid, however, the thin and stringy growth of summer. Both leaves and stems are good to eat when young and fresh. Scissors are a must when collecting this plant, otherwise you will uproot the entire plant, tough stems, roots, mud and all. Watch out for any entwining speedwell plants which are superficially similar but nearly always show their distinctive tiny blue flowers.

Chickweed is easily distinguished from potential impostors, such as the larger and slightly edible Greater Stitchwort (*Stellaria holostea*), by the single line of fine hairs running the length of the stem.

The flavour is mild and pleasant, not unlike lettuce but with a bit of freshly mown cricket pitch thrown in. It is fine in a salad as long as only the youngest stems are used. It works well in a soup and makes for an excellent stir-fry, but my favourite recipe is for Chickweed Pakoras (p.211).

Single line of fine hairs on stem

Common Mallow *Malva sylvestris*

DESCRIPTION	Medium annual/perennial, 0.8–1.5 metres, usually upright. Leaves rounded palmate (palm-shaped), lower leaves more rounded, often with a central dark spot, downy/hairy, on long stem. Flowers five-petalled, pink/mauve. Seeds in a ring like a ring doughnut
HABITAT	Roadside, waste ground, field edge. Frequently coastal
DISTRIBUTION	Very common throughout much of the British Isles but scarcer in northern England, Scotland and Wales. Very scarce in Northern Ireland
SEASON	Spring for the leaves, though they can be found through much of the year. Late summer for the seeds

The marshmallows we buy today were once, of course, made from the mucilaginous roots of real marsh-mallows. But this is quite a rare plant these days, found only in the upper reaches of some marshes and in brackish ditches from the Wash southwards. Common Mallow, however, is what it says it is – common. I do not think you will be making any sweetmeats from this plant as the roots are too small, but the leaves and the little seeds are edible.

The mucilage found in its leaves has given this plant its reputation as a soothing plant rather like aloe vera. Culpeper prescribes it for scaldings, burnings, swellings, dandruff and, most worrying of all, excoriations of the bowels. And also for '*the stinging of bees, wasps and the like*'. One of its old names is Round Dock, and it may be Common Mallow that we should rub on Stinging Nettle rashes not Common Dock.

The mildly nutty seeds were once commonly eaten by children, but they are fiddly to collect and it is primarily the leaves that are used. Common Mallow can be found easily everywhere, particularly near the sea. The young leaves of spring are certainly the best, but even these will pick up a considerable amount of dust on their slightly furry surface. Just wash them well before cooking. Mallow leaves start to wilt the moment they are picked, so seal them in a plastic box to take them home.

The flavour is mild and pleasant, and the texture slightly slimy. As a plain vegetable it is a non-starter, though I did make a slightly slippery bubble and squeak with it once. There is really only one 'proper' thing that can be made from the Common Mallow – the Middle Eastern dish, Molukhia or Jew's Mallow soup. It is not a complicated dish, consisting mostly of chicken meat, chicken stock, garlic and lots of finely chopped Common Mallow leaves. It looks a little like 'grass-cutting' soup to me but tastes good.

Fat Hen *Chenopodium album*

DESCRIPTION	Upright, medium annual, to 1 metre. Leaves very variable but roughly rounded triangular, narrower at top of mature stem, covered in white meal – especially when young, feel slightly greasy. Flowers grow from leaf joints on spikes
HABITAT	Disturbed, cultivated ground. Compost heaps. Not on high ground
DISTRIBUTION	Extremely common throughout the British Isles, but rare in the east of Scotland
SEASON	May–October

Having some years ago been evicted from my allotment for taking an over-relaxed view of cultivation, it is still nice to visit the old place from time to time to see how my more diligent successors are getting on. Of course it is not just nostalgia that draws me there – it is the weeds. Chief among these is Fat Hen. Any piece of nitrogen-rich cultivated ground, left for a couple of weeks in the summer, can start to sprout a perfect crop of this tasty vegetable. Being a generous sort and not wanting to keep it all for myself I tell the gardeners that it is edible and tasty, but they always proceed to dig it in and, with much labour, plant the inferior spinach instead.

Fat Hen has been around for millennia but was probably introduced and, like so many other once-popular plants, has overstayed its welcome. It was used as a favourite green vegetable until a few centuries ago when it was replaced by the related spinach. The seeds can last in the soil for decades; there appear to be four different varieties, all with different germination requirements and longevity, and seed densities can reach tens of thousands per square metre. It is a persistent and troublesome weed not just in allotment gardens but also on agricultural land, where much effort is expended in suppressing it. The forager, of course, cares not for the woes of others and this information just tells him or her where to look.

Fat Hen is easy to identify once you have the hang of it. It is, unfortunately, rather variable in its appearance (*morphological plasticity*, don't you know) and it hybridises with other members of the goosefoot family, which already look like it anyway. Furthermore, the young plants and leaves look unlike the mature plants and leaves. None of this would matter too much if there was nothing nasty to confuse it with but, inevitably, there is. These are members of the treacherous Solanaceae (potato family) such as Black Nightshade and Datura. The safest way to be sure you have Fat Hen is to pick the young plants at 15cm or so, with their more

Red Goosefoot

highly distinctive mealy surface, or the fully grown ones, with their unmistakable flower spikes. Two or three crops of young plants a year are easily available from the same piece of land if it is dug over after picking (this counts as gardening if you do it yourself and foraging if someone else does it). You should never be short of Fat Hen between May and October.

The flavour is similar to spinach but a little less bitter, and can be used in similar situations. The delicate leaves do not steam well and are best sweated with a little butter for 5 minutes. Hen Chicken (p.215) is a good way of using a substantial amount of Fat Hen in a tasty dish. I suggest serving it with a salad of Chickweed.

Also look out for quite a large number of other goosefoots. These are members of the goosefoot genus (*Chenopodium*), not necessarily the overarching goosefoot family (*Chenopodiaceae*), which also includes the edible Sea Beet and Marsh Samphire. Principal among these is Red Goosefoot (*C. rubrum*). The leaves of this plant are unhappily like those of some nightshades, so do be careful and wait until the flower spikes start to appear if you are unsure (the nightshades have five-petalled and often rather flamboyant flowers). The leaves are unusually shiny for a goosefoot. The stem normally exhibits a red coloration in amongst the green, as do the flowers. By far the best place to find this neat plant is on a compost heap.

The best-known goosefoot, other than Fat Hen, is Good King Henry (*C. bonus-henricus*); sadly it is now a fairly uncommon plant though it was once extensively cultivated. The strange name, repeated in the Latin epithet, is from the German *Guter Heinrich*. Heinrich was probably an elf and the 'Good' part was to differentiate the plant from the unrelated and poisonous 'Bad Henry' – Dog's Mercury. Quite where the 'King' bit comes from no one knows.

Further than this, there are over thirty other goosefoots in the British Isles. Fig-leaved Goosefoot, Many-seeded Goosefoot and Nettle-leaved Goosefoot are all fairly common and all with a roughly southern and eastern distribution; most of the rest are extremely rare. It is likely that nearly all are more or less edible, though Foetid Goosefoot and Stinking Goosefoot do not sound too promising.

Spear-leaved Orache *Atriplex prostrata*

DESCRIPTION	Medium annual, to 1 metre. Often upright, but seaside plants especially can be straggling. Lower leaves fairly large, triangular with straight base approximately at right angles to the leaf stem, broadly toothed, slightly mealy. Upper leaves narrow on maturity. Flowers grow on spikes from leaf joints
HABITAT	Waste ground, cultivated ground, compost heaps, upper beaches
DISTRIBUTION	Very common in England, though rare in the Northwest. Coastal elsewhere
SEASON	May–October

I find Spear-leaved Orache more often than its relative Fat Hen. It too can be found in cultivated soil and waste ground, but Spear-leaved Orache also has a holiday home by the sea. Sometimes you will find a substantial crop in an unusual place; my best find of this plant was underneath the steps at Dorchester South Railway Station – there was also a nice patch of Wild Strawberries just outside the main entrance and I nearly missed my train.

As with other members of the goosefoot family, this plant does have certain similarities to the Solanaceae family, the nightshades. Black Nightshade, for example, has similar-shaped leaves but lacks, among other things, the distinctly straight base to its triangular leaves. One plant you will almost certainly confuse it with, given the chance, is Good King Henry. This is much less common, shorter, its leaves are less lobed and it has a different flower structure – apart from that there is little between them so it is just as well that it too is edible.

All the oraches mentioned here are good spinach substitutes though too bitter to be used raw in a salad.

Also look out for several other oraches, Common Orache (*A. patula*) being the most obvious. Again it is a weed of cultivation with a liking for the seaside. Babington's Orache (*A. glabriuscula*) and Frosted Orache (*A. laciniata*) are exclusively seaside plants, often forming long mats of vegetation above the strand-line. The first has small triangular/oval leaves; the second does what it says it does and looks as though it is covered in frost.

If you are confused by the oraches and the goosefoots then I welcome you to a not very exclusive club. Even my most enthusiastic botanical friends despair at giving a positive identification for many of them. Serious floras, such as the excellent *New Flora of the British Isles* by Clive Stace, has for one of the goosefoots '... *lower leaves trullate to triangular-ovate, acute to rounded, and mucronate at apex, cunate to truncate at base...*' and so on. For the forager the main thing to know is that they *are* oraches or goosefoots – most are good to eat and none will do you any harm. All those mentioned here have some degree of mealiness on the leaves and tiny flowers which grow in long spikes originating from where the leaf joins the stem.

Wood Sorrel *Oxalis acetosella*

DESCRIPTION	Low creeping perennial. Leaves trefoil, leaflets heart-shaped with central fold, finely hairy, yellowish green. Stems red/brown. Leaf and flower stems *unbranched* and arising from a single base. Flowers five-petalled, white to pale pink with mauve veins, yellow centres. Carpeting woodland floor. All parts taste acidic
HABITAT	All types of woods including coniferous; shady places
DISTRIBUTION	Very common throughout the British Isles, except the Fens
SEASON	All year, though best in the spring and early summer

Wood Sorrel is a refined and delicate plant, quite unlike its rough grassland namesake, Sorrel. The flavour, however, is the same – powerfully acidic. Found all over the country, it can carpet the woodland floor with pretty leaves which fold up at night like automatic origami. *Oxalis* comes from the Greek *oxys* meaning 'sharp' (oxygen has the same derivation though unjustified, due to the mistaken belief that it is essential for making acids; a job done, in fact, by hydrogen). The name Sorrel is also a reference to the taste, being derived from *sur*, the French for 'sour'.

The trefoil nature of the leaves has made it one of the candidates for the shamrock, with which St Patrick demonstrated the nature of the Holy Trinity (in fact the Trinity is a mystery and resists metaphor). Another familiar religious association is due to its flowering at Easter time, giving it the occasional name of Alleluia.

The flowers are unusual in that while they are nearly always infertile, the plant always sets seed. In fact the seeds are produced by tiny, unopening and self-fertile flowers near the roots in a process called cleistogamy ('closed marriage' – 'open marriage', if you're wondering, is called chasmogamy). The visible flowers are, it seems, just for show.

Many people confuse Wood Sorrel with clover. This is a terrible novice mistake to make and will cause you much embarrassment on any natural history society ramble. Clover leaflets are oval, never heart-shaped. An easier, and more dangerous, error is confusion with the related Procumbent Yellow Sorrel (*Oxalis corniculata*). This contains potentially dangerous levels of oxalic acid and has caused deaths in grazing animals if not in humans. Its stems are branched, the flowers are yellow and it seldom grows in woods, so you should have no trouble with it.

It is pleasantly refreshing on a hot spring day to nibble a few leaves of Wood Sorrel, but if you want more, then scissors will be needed to avoid bringing the woodland floor home with you too. The plant is tiny and it does take a while to collect a reasonable amount. A newspaper report complaining about commercial collecting and the fairly substantial price obtainable for a kilo of Wood Sorrel showed not the slightest inkling of how long such a quantity would take to collect – about a day in my opinion.

The stems and flowers are edible as well as the leaves, with the same lemony grape-skin flavour. Although it is available almost all year, the fresh growth of the spring is better flavoured and textured.

As it is attractive, Wood Sorrel is sometimes used as a decorative and fruity garnish. I once used it (rather daringly, I thought) on a lemon torte. It is a perfect alternative to lemon with fish, either alone or in a mixed wild salad. (It is worth mentioning here that not all wild salads work – I once tried Wood Sorrel, Ramsons and Hairy Bittercress all together – it was unspeakably vile.)

Wood Sorrel can also be made into an excellent sauce by chopping the leaves finely, then sweating them in some double cream for a couple of minutes – just perfect with salmon or trout.

The taste of Wood Sorrel comes from oxalic acid and calcium oxalate, which are poisonous but present in Wood Sorrel in sufficiently small quantities to be harmless unless you eat a great deal. See entry for Sorrel (p.110).

Broom *Cytisus scoparius*

DESCRIPTION	Wiry shrub up to 2 metres. Lower leaves small trefoil. Stems spineless, angular in section, green. Flowers brilliant yellow, like tiny sweetpeas when open
HABITAT	Heath, roadsides, open woods. Often on sand
DISTRIBUTION	Common throughout the British Isles, except the Fens and northwestern extremity of Scotland
SEASON	Buds from April until early June

Geoffrey Count of Anjou, father of Henry II, wore a sprig of Broom as an emblem. The medieval Latin name of the Broom is *Planta genista* and is the origin of Plantagenet. This is the sort of story that will make you the centre of attention at parties and is worth remembering.

There are several flowers that can be eaten on their own and Broom buds are the most accessible of them all. The shrub is visible for some miles on a sunny day because of the dazzling intensity of its yellow flowers. The related and unpalatable gorse has furry buds and spiny leaves. Broom buds (the bright-yellow but unopened flower) are available in the spring and are best when small and tight.

Broom is in the pea family so it is little surprise that the flavour is that of pea, or perhaps another relative, the runner bean. They provide a tasty decoration on a spring salad and can be added to a stir-fry at the last moment. You can also pickle them, if you must.

My recommendation of Broom is wholehearted, but comes with two small warnings. All parts of the Broom, including the flower buds, contain trace amounts of toxins – sparteine and isosparteine being chief among them. These can depress heart function, cause paralysis and restrict peripheral blood vessels. You may need to eat around two kilograms of the buds before noticing the effects, so a dozen on a wild green salad are unlikely to do you any harm. Rarely, you might encounter the Spanish Broom (*Spartium junceum*), distinguished by its pine-like leaves. The buds of this Broom contain significantly higher levels of toxin and must not be eaten.

P.S. There are a few other wild flowers that can be used for their decorative qualities – Bramble, Rose and Borage on a salad, or Primroses set on top of a Champagne jelly. Primroses can even be candied by brushing on a strong sugar solution and letting them dry. Sweet Violets, if you can find them, may also be preserved in this way. (A piece of advice to any male readers who tread this floral path is not to tell your mates about it in the pub.)

Blackberry *Rubus fruticosus* agg.

DESCRIPTION	Scrambling, arching shrub, to 3 metres. Leaves with three to five leaflets – oval/pointed, serrated edge, hairy white underside. Stem with backward-pointing strong, sharp thorns. Flowers five-petalled, white to pale pink. Fruit consisting of many dark purple/black segments
HABITAT	Woods, hedgerows, waste ground, gardens. All soil types, but does not like very wet conditions
DISTRIBUTION	Extremely common throughout the British Isles, except the Scottish Highlands
SEASON	Berries from August until mid-October

Plants often possess a distinct personality but few have one quite as large as that of the common Blackberry. This untidy, sprawling, invasive shrub is self-confident to the point of boorishness, yet more generous than any other plant in this book. Foraging for fruit can be hard work – the Redcurrant and the Raspberry, the Wild Strawberry and the Bilberry are all difficult to find in any quantity – but the Blackberry may be regularly picked by the bucketful.

My record for one season's Blackberry picking is 65 kilograms (it was a good year for field mushrooms, too, with 50 kilograms from the field just above the Blackberry patch). Such quantities are not unusual and the imagination and operational schedule of the cook can be taxed to the limit. Of course there is always the freezer – but they can languish there neglected and forgotten for years (I once inherited several ancient bags of Blackberries from a friend who was emigrating).

No one has any trouble identifying a Blackberry – it is something we seem almost born to recognise; the only berry that will cause confusion is the very similar and equally edible Dewberry. Finding them will also not be hard. As Gerard says, '*The bramble groweth for the most part in every hedge and bush*' and it is indeed common in hedgerows everywhere, odd corners of farms, scrub, woodland, unruly gardens and waste ground. It is the one plant that the town-dwelling forager will always be able to find – usually in otherwise unattractive corners of the urban environment.

Few people will have missed out on the singular pleasures of Blackberry picking – it is something nearly every child has, or should have, done at some time. I did once go Blackberry picking with a young lady for whom these fruit were things that came in ready-made pies. She wore medical latex gloves to protect her hands from contamination with the real world. They lasted 4 seconds but she still survived to tell of her ordeal.

I recall the Blackberry-picking trips of my childhood. These were military operations involving unseasonably thick clothing, leather gloves, baskets and buckets, and a search of the house for the walking stick with a crook on the end. I recommend this sort of preparation if you want to pick in quantity. There is much to be said for using one leather-gloved hand to hold the stalk, and the other ungloved hand to pick the berries. A walking stick to hook out-of-reach bunches and beat down the undergrowth is essential. Long sleeves and Wellington boots will protect you from most of the vicious thorns, though you will be very lucky to get away completely unscathed. The late August and early September days that form the peak of the Blackberry season are also a good time for the flies that infest both them and you. Blackberrying, as I am sure you know, is a very uncomfortable enterprise but worth every single scratch.

There is a well-known superstition that Blackberries should not be picked after Michaelmas because the Devil has spat on them, fallen on them (having been cast out of heaven on that day), thrown his cloak over them or stamped on them. Michaelmas is 29 September or, if you use the old calendar, 10 October. The best Blackberries tend to be early in the season when the sun is strong, before the flies have pierced them and the grey mould *Botrytis cinerea* has taken hold. But there is no genuine reason for not picking them late in the year, so long as you can find good ones.

The biggest and sweetest berry is usually the one at the end of the stalk. This ripens long before all the others and is the one to eat raw; the rest are best for cooking. Quite what a Blackberry will taste like is a bit of an unknown until you actually eat it. Ripeness and weather seem to have a large bearing, but the Blackberry comes in many microspecies, which may vary greatly in taste.

Blackberries do not keep. Not even for a day. The mould spores are sat on the surface of the berries waiting to do their worst, so whatever it is that you hope to make with your precious cache you should start straight away. If there is no time to make your jam or crumble, at least cook the berries through by simmering them on a low heat for a few minutes.

The sheer quantity of Blackberries that you can collect opens up possibilities that would be wasteful or impractical with other berries. The best country wine I've made was Blackberry, and the best jelly I ever made – well, that was Blackberry too. Blackberry jelly, vinegar, sorbet or ice cream, Blackberry and apple pie or crumble, summer pudding and fruit leather – I could list a hundred ways of cooking this adaptable fruit, but many will already be familiar to you. Three ideas from three giants of the hedgerow harvest are, however, of particular note. Hugh adapts a Sloe Gin recipe to make a Blackberry whisky, which gets better and better with keeping if you have the self-restraint to allow it to. Richard Mabey tells us of Blackberry 'junket', made by keeping the juice of ripe berries in a warm room overnight until it sets, and Pam Corbin has the perfect recipe for Bramble Mousse (p.221).

Crab Apple *Malus sylvestris*

DESCRIPTION	Small tree. Leaves broadly oval/pointed, toothed edge, alternate. Twigs and branches intricately entangled, true Crab Apple trees quite often have occasional thorns
HABITAT	Woods, hedgerows
DISTRIBUTION	Common in England south of Cumbria and in lowland Wales and Scotland, uncommon elsewhere
SEASON	September–October

A fully burdened Crab Apple tree is a wonderful sight in autumn, but chiefly from a distance. The apples themselves are, as one Edward Long put it in the eighteenth century, '*never admired for loveliness of aspect*'. Small, misshapen, spotty and scabby, and full of pips, they do not inspire the cook. Nor are they remotely edible raw – they must be cooked. Yet when prepared properly they are a treasure.

Old woodland and farm hedges away from habitation are the most likely places to find the true Crab Apple. Roadside trees are much more likely to have arisen from discarded pips – 'wildings' as they are called. The Crab Apple has a malleable genetic makeup, which has allowed it to be developed into the two thousand or so domesticated apple varieties that exist today. A tree grown from the pip of a cultivated apple can produce a totally unpredictable fruit. It may be similar to its parent apple; often it will be just like a Crab Apple, or sometimes it will be completely different from either. The forager must always take a pragmatic view of what is on offer. Apples growing on any wild tree – whether true Crab Apple or wilding – must be judged solely on their merits, not on their racial purity.

The true Crab Apple is a fine fruit with some useful qualities. Chief among these is the sharpness which makes it inedible raw. This is principally down to the tongue-dissolving malic acid, beloved of 'extreme candy' eaters. Verjuice is a venerable substitute for lemon juice or vinegar, which exploits this quality well. (The name, incidentally, comes from the French *verde* or 'green', most verjuice being made from under-ripe grapes.) It can also be produced from apples that have been left in a pile for a month to mature; those that have matured too far are discarded and the remaining apples mashed and pressed. The juice is kept for a few weeks to mature a little more, then bottled. The intensely sharp flavour makes it a particularly good accompaniment to fish.

I use Crab Apples in an (almost) entirely wild version of Pam Corbin's 'leathers'. Hawthorn and Crab Apple Leather is a first-class way of dealing with two fruits that

are mostly pips and skin. To prepare, chop 500g Crab Apples and stew with 500g Haws and 100ml water for 20 minutes. Push the cooked mixture through a fine sieve into a saucepan, add 150g sugar and heat the pulp, stirring until the sugar dissolves. Now spread the purée on baking trays lined with baking parchment and place in a low oven (at 50–60°C/Gas mark ⅛) for 12–18 hours until dry and leathery.

Of course, the recipe for which this tart apple is best known is Crab Apple jelly. The very high pectin content means that it will always set well, and other fruits can be added to make a variety of jellies. Cooked, strained and with sugar added, Crab Apples also make a sharp apple sauce – just use extra sugar if it takes the roof of your mouth off. Although Crab Apples are not very lovely whole, they can still be used sliced as decoration, as in Cranberry and Apple Tart (p.222).

P.S. I cannot resist passing on this medicinal recipe from the early 1800s; it is for a concoction called Black Drop:

> *Take half a pound of opium sliced, three parts of good verjuice, one and a half ounces of nutmeg, and half an ounce of saffron. Boil them to a proper thickness; then add a quarter of a pound of sugar, and two spoonfuls of yeast. Set the whole in a warm place near the fire for six or eight weeks, then place it in the open air, until it become a syrup; lastly, decant, filter, bottle it up, adding a little sugar to each bottle.*

I am not sure what it was supposed to cure; everything perhaps.

Hawthorn *Crataegus monogyna*

DESCRIPTION	Shrub or small tree. Leaves with deeply divided lobes, stalked, pair of stipules (tiny leaves) at the base. Spiny branches. Flowers in sprays, five white petals, stamens pink. Berries red, like miniature apples, single large seed
HABITAT	Hedgerow, or occasionally singly as well-shaped trees
DISTRIBUTION	Very common everywhere, except the north of Scotland
SEASON	Flowers May–June, berries August–November or even December

The Hawthorn is Britain's most abundant hedgerow tree. Millions were planted as dividing hedges to fulfil the eighteenth- and nineteenth-century Inclosure Acts. A bright legacy of a tragic past. From the middle of May until June, Hawthorn's heady and dazzling 'May' blossom enlivens the countryside and from August to November its rich red berries are the very stuff of autumn.

This humble tree has more folklore and tradition associated with it than any other plant, save perhaps the Elder, and I recommend Richard Mabey's *Flora Britannica* and Geoffrey Grigson's *Englishman's Flora* for full expositions. Chief among its associations are those constant preoccupations – love (or to be frank, sex) and death. The love bit owes something to the tree's flamboyant springtime fecundity though mostly it is the smell – heady and fragrant, but also with a strangely moving undertone, trimethylamine. This chemical is one of the first products of putrefaction (most familiarly of fish), leading the pessimistically inclined to connect the blossom with death, while the optimistic mind turns to a more cheering association.

You will certainly have no trouble finding May blossoms or Haws (the usual troublesome name for the berries), with only the rounder-leaved Midland Hawthorn likely to cause any confusion. This is less common but can be used in the kitchen in the same way, although the blossom is very potent indeed. Hawthorn is in the apple sub-family, as a cursory look at either flower or berry will tell you. Another member – the much-cultivated and sometimes naturalised cotoneaster – may confuse the extremely unobservant, but it has quite different leaves. Nevertheless, do familiarise yourself with the poisonous red berries described later in this book if you are at all unsure. As with most of the plants that provide both flower and berry, pick the flower early and the berry late. Flowers about to drop will have lost their perfume and early berries will be low in sugar and flavour.

Another crop available from the tree is the young leaves. These are the 'bread' of 'bread and cheese' collected by country children, though very much in the past. The

'cheese' is the unopened flower buds. Many people say they like them and they are entitled to do so; however, in common with all other leaves of trees, what little flavour they possess is pretty awful.

If you can come to amicable terms with the superstition that bringing May blossom into the house is bad luck you will be able to make Wild Flower Syrup (p.237). This is very similar to maple syrup and considerably cheaper. If you are concerned about the slightly indecent smell, it does disappear, well almost.

The berries are a bit of a challenge to the forager. There are so many of them – it must amount to millions of tons a year – yet they are time-consuming (and prickly) to pick and not easy to use. The flavour of the flesh is mildly fruity and slightly starchy – like an over-ripe apple. They are not particularly pleasant eaten raw and consist largely of pip. Cooking, therefore, is the only course of action. They will make a passable jelly when mixed with apples, a good wine and an excellent sauce (see Pam Corbin's *River Cottage Preserves Handbook*). However, the best way of doing justice to their sheer numbers is to make a fruit leather (p.69).

P.S. Hawthorn leaves, eaten on the hoof or in a mixed salad, are not that bad, though I have given them to adults who are always disappointed with the taste which is not at all what they remember from their childhood. A few tree leaves are edible – Beech, Hawthorn and Lime being the best known. I have managed to eat Oak leaves when extremely young (them, not me) and sometimes they are nice enough, at other times mouth-numbingly bitter. Lime is the best of them, having good-flavoured young leaves with a decidedly mucilaginous texture. Beech leaves? Don't bother.

Rowan *Sorbus aucuparia*

DESCRIPTION	Small tree. Leaves pinnate (lots of leaflets, like an ash tree), with many opposite leaflets and one terminal leaflet. Blossom in umbrella sprays, white, with an unpleasant smell. Berries bright red
HABITAT	Often solitary in hilly or mountainous areas to nearly 1000 metres. Planted in urban areas. Uncommon with lime
DISTRIBUTION	Common in suitable habitats throughout the British Isles
SEASON	Berries August–November

This little tree is one of our hardiest plants, happy to cling to precipitous mountain-sides and at a higher altitude than any tree other than the Juniper. Not that you will have to put on your climbing boots to find one – it can easily be found in lowland heath and wood, and is a frequently planted suburban tree.

Most of our native trees have some magical associations, but it is usually the smaller ones that are considered the most powerful. The Elder and the Hawthorn are two such trees and the Rowan is a third; perhaps it is due to their more human size. It is likely that the name Rowan is a reference to the dazzling colour of the early-autumn tree when both berry and leaf turn red; Rowan may simply mean

'red-one'. Red is the colour of protection and it is for this property that Rowan is planted outside dwellings. In *The Laidly Worm of Spindleston Heugh* (a tale of a Northumberland dragon) we learn:

> *Their spells were vain. The hags return'd*
> *To the Queen in sorrowful mood,*
> *Crying that witches have no power,*
> *Where there is Rown-Tree wood.*

Even in Northumberland, neither witches nor dragons are the problem they once were, but it is still an attractive tree to have in the garden. If it has a failing, it is the smell of the blossom – it smells of rotting flesh.

Identification of the Rowan is simple while the ash-like leaves are still in place. Unfortunately the berries are commonly picked quite late in the year and the leaves may have long gone. The answer is to select your trees before the leaves fall. Whitebeam produces very similar berries on a very similar tree but has totally different-shaped leaves. Fortunately the berries are not poisonous.

It is a pity that so common and productive a tree has not seen fit to grow berries of a better flavour, but the fact is they are both tart and bitter, and full of pips. They are also poisonous raw. Cooking does little to reduce the bitter quality, so even something like a Rowan and apple tart is likely to be less than delicious. As a soft fruit it is therefore something of a failure but, of course, it has one use which rescues it from foraging oblivion – Rowan jelly. Again I will refer you to Pam Corbin's *River Cottage Preserves Handbook*, where a full recipe for a doubly wild jelly (it also contains Crab Apples) is given.

P.S. In 2006, in an episode that defies irony, a gentleman in his sixties from Gloucestershire reportedly climbed over a fence on to private land while on a walk in Cheshire and picked some Rowan berries. There were, it seems, words spoken between the picker and a security guard from a nearby building who had spotted the misdemeanour and had remonstrated. Three months later, back in Gloucestershire, the local police, having been notified of the putative felon's address by the Cheshire constabulary (who themselves discovered it from CCTV footage of the gentleman's car), called on the berry-picker and took him to the police station. He admitted an offence under the 1968 Theft Act and accepted a caution.

It is unclear whether or not this was a miscarriage of justice. If the Rowan berries were cultivated – and it has been said that they were 'cultivated' as food for birds – then it was theft. If they were growing wild, then under the 1968 Theft Act it was most definitely not. The berry-picker's wife made half a dozen jars of Rowan jelly from the berries, making the principle of law '*de minimis non curat lex*' – 'The law does not concern itself with trifles'– doubly appropriate.

Silverweed *Potentilla anserina*

DESCRIPTION	Short, creeping perennial with runners. Leaflets with saw-toothed edge, silvery due to fine hairs, at least on the underside. Flowers yellow, five-petalled
HABITAT	With grass, waste ground, garden borders
DISTRIBUTION	Very common throughout the UK
SEASON	Roots best dug in late summer and autumn. Leaves visible from spring until mid-October

The old name for Silverweed was Wild Tansy. The 'other' tansy has similarly shaped leaves but is unrelated and a member of the daisy family. Culpeper notes this, saying:

> *Now Dame Venus hath fitted women with two herbs of the same name, the one to help conception, and the other to maintain beauty, and what more can be expected of her?*

What indeed? Silverweed performs the first function, being the '… *best companion their husbands excepted*' that a woman desiring a child might have.

Silverweed is related to the various cinquefoils and to the familiar tormentil, and is in the rose family. Its Latin name *Potentilla* means 'little powerful one' and it certainly seems to survive just about anywhere. There is never any problem finding such a tough little plant and you will probably have some in your garden as a persistent weed of your flower borders. The edible roots can be dug up at any time of the year but it is best to do so after they have put on weight during the summer and certainly before the leaves have died completely and you can't find them. This is any time from September to mid-October. The leaves are very distinctive with their saw-toothed edges and silvery coating of hairs. Digging them up will reveal a mass of roots, not all of which will be Silverweed, so do be careful. A good Silverweed root will have nodules along its length and may be the thickness of a French bean.

It is fair to say that unless you have absolutely nothing else to do, digging up Silverweed roots is not necessarily the best use of your time. They have long been considered a famine food, but as famine foods go, they are really rather good. The flavour is of chestnuts or perhaps Jerusalem artichokes; they are just very fiddly to collect and prepare. Times can change of course and in post-apocalyptic Britain you may yet save your tribe with the arcane knowledge imparted here.

Use a nylon scouring pad or knife to remove the skin and then boil, steam or sauté them. In the past, a flour has been ground from the dried roots, and pancakes made from this, though that really would be wasting your time.

Silverweed roots and leaves

Sloe/Blackthorn *Prunus spinosa*

DESCRIPTION	Shrub or small tree. Leaves oval, toothed. Trunk and branches dark brown to almost black, long, tough, sharp thorns. Flowers white with red stamens, five-petalled, appearing in March before the leaves. Fruit 1–1.5cm, dark blue/purple/black, with a bloom
HABITAT	Wood edges, scrub, hedgerow
DISTRIBUTION	Very common throughout the British Isles, though increasingly scarce in the north of Scotland
SEASON	September–November, sometimes in December

Most foragers have a secret Sloe patch of which they speak proudly and guard zealously. As one who lives in an area in which the Blackthorn seems to be the dominant shrub and who can pick 50 kilograms before breakfast, I shake my head disdainfully at such talk. Not that I am without pity for those less fortunate.

With its almost black bark of winter, white blossom of spring and grape-like fruit of autumn, the Blackthorn is a lovely tree. It can fill a hedgerow or form dense, impenetrable thickets, providing a safe nesting site for many bird species. The blossom is the earliest in the year (except for that of the closely related Cherry Plum), appearing and usually falling before the leaves are unfurled. A very excitable nineteenth-century traveller, one William Anderson, described the berries in prose more purple than they themselves are: '*distilled in tears… ethereal globules; now blue… now black, with the play of the raven's wing…*'

Along with the Plums, the Blackthorn is a member of the genus *Prunus*, in turn a member of the rose family, the Rosaceae. The second half of its Latin name is clear enough in meaning if you have ever had a close encounter with a Blackthorn. The spines are vicious in the extreme, seemingly designed to kill rather than deter. Indeed they were once considered to be poisonous, since the wounds they inflict often refuse to heal.

Following the blossom and an inconspicuous few months, August sees the new berries forming. These green acid drops are quite inedible, though at one time the juice was squeezed from them and slowly boiled dry to form *Acacia Germanica*. It was said (without risk of exaggeration – it must have tasted like battery acid) to be a powerful astringent and was '*given in fluxes, etc. from a scruple to a dram*'. The acidity of Sloes is down to our old friend malic acid, but there is also tartaric acid and tannic acid, the latter chemical being the one responsible for sticking your tongue to the roof of your mouth.

The mouth-numbing properties of even the ripest berry is familiar to most, and the longer you can leave the berries on the tree the better. A mild and wet November can, however, ripen them to a plump softness and raw edibility, at least for the stout hearted. October is probably the time when most people pick them, though I have on occasion found them persisting until Christmas. The berries form in huge numbers around the branches and would be fairly easy to pick were it not for those terrible thorns. At least one gardening glove should be used when gathering Sloes and a hat would be a wise addition to protect your head.

Although there are several delicious things that can be made with Sloes the word that twins with it most often is gin. There seem to be as many methods for making this simple liqueur as there are people who make it and I did some selfless research one Christmas, going around my village tasting as many recipes and vintages as I could talk people into giving me. Unfortunately I did not take notes and have unaccountably forgotten the details beyond the fact that they were all 'jolly nice'. However, one thing about Sloe Gin, which I knew already, was amply confirmed – the older the vintage, the better it is. The best one I tried was fourteen years old – it was like a fine Madeira.

The basic recipe could not be simpler: Prick 500g Sloes with a fork and place them in a large jar. Add 500g sugar and 600ml gin. Shake to mix everything up and give the jar a further shake every now and then over the next week, at least. It will be just about drinkable after a couple of months but if you can keep it for the next year it will be much improved. If you decide to keep it, then remove the Sloes after 3 months.

The only other familiar recipe for this fruit is Sloe and Crab Apple jelly. A jam is also possible if you sieve out the pits from the well-cooked Sloes; unless you use a pectinised sugar you will need to add the same weight of cooked Crab Apples (or cooking apples) to provide the pectin it needs to set. Finally, there is the excellent standby for any fruit that needs straining to remove pips or pits – a fruit leather.

P.S. Sloes form an important ingredient in a heroic recipe from the *Family Save-all* of 1861. It also contains Elderberry juice, so it would make an appropriate forager's nip (or bath):

> *Take twelve gallons of soft river water, forty-eight pounds of raisins, fourteen
> pounds of Lisbon sugar, twelve quarts of elder juice, three quarts of juice of sloes,
> and half an ounce of isinglass; mix all together; when this has stood two months,
> or till it is fine, draw it off into a clear cask, and add six pounds of loaf sugar
> and three quarts of brandy. Bottle it in the April following, and keep it two years
> before drawing the corks.*

Wild Cherry *Prunus avium*

DESCRIPTION	Small to medium tree. Leaves long, pointed oval, saw-toothed edge. Blossom white and abundant. Fruit generally smaller than cultivated varieties, hanging down on *separate* stalks
HABITAT	Woodland edges and occasionally in hedgerows. Often planted in streets and along dual carriageways, etc.
DISTRIBUTION	Frequent throughout the British Isles, though less common in the North and parts of the west of Scotland
SEASON	Late June and July

Beautiful berries! Beautiful tree! Hurrah! for the wild, wild cherry tree' go the enthusiastic if slightly awkward lines of a nineteenth-century song. The sentiments at least are ones with which we can concur.

There are several varieties of Cherry that grow wild in the British Isles, but the native Wild Cherry is the one most likely to produce useful fruit. The modern cultivated varieties are largely its descendants, crossed and selected over the years to produce heavier and sweeter fruit. The 'wild' Wild Cherry is usually found as a forest tree but it does like the light and normally clings to the wood edge.

Cherry pits travel around a great deal and some of the more productive roadside trees will be the result of felicitous littering. The best Wild Cherry trees I know were actually planted by the Highways Agency on the steeply sloping banks of a local bypass, though they make for rather dangerous foraging. I take an entirely pragmatic view of collecting this lovely fruit; if the tree is growing more or less wild and produces decent Cherries, I will pick them – provenance does not concern me. Cherries do grow on trees of course, so you may need to engage in a little climbing, adding to the experience rather than detracting from it, and the 'standing on the roof of the car' technique (p.15) can be very useful.

'*Oh where is a wild cherry tree?*' If you do not know of any Wild Cherry trees in your area keep your eyes open for the flamboyant April blossom that has overexcited poets for centuries: '*… what are those living hills of snow, or of some substance purer in its brightness even than any snow that falls…?*' The fruit will start to appear at the end of June and you will have to be quick to beat the birds. Normally it is necessary to pick slightly under-ripe fruit and ripen them at home; though, as the picture overleaf shows, sometimes you can be lucky. Like other *Prunus* species, such as Plums, the fruit is variable in quality – '*grateful to the Stomach, and whet the Appetite*', as one writer has it, or '*harsh and crude to the taste*', according to another – you will just have to pick and taste.

Wild Cherries are relatively small, but can be used in all the recipes devised for their cultivated cousins. The strong acidity of some of the wild fruit lends itself to glacé cherries (the home-made ones put the commercial variety to shame). Sweet Cherry Pickle is quick and easy: simply pit the Cherries, pack them in a clean jar and cover with a mix of hot, lightly spiced cider vinegar and sugar to taste. You can also make a jam, though take care – Cherry jam is one I regularly manage to burn before it sets. Best of all, and most likely to do justice to your hard-won cherries, is Wild Cherry brandy – just replace all the appropriate ingredients in the recipe for Sloe Gin (p.82).

P.S. When I am not out foraging, I work as a cabinet maker. I cannot therefore talk about Cherry without mentioning its wood. Cherry is one of the finest cabinet making woods in existence, rivalling mahogany in its depth of colour and grain but without the accompanying concerns about rainforest destruction. Sadly most Cherry trees are too scattered for commercial harvesting, ending their lives as logs (though very good logs), their potential for becoming a chair or table lost for ever. The wood is fairly easy to work, though the grain often changes direction several times over the length of a plank and planing is necessarily done against the grain with a finely set and extremely sharp blade. The most noticeable thing about cherry wood is that when it becomes overheated during machining it smells of Cherries.

P.P.S. Cherry-pit is an old game involving throwing stones or cherry pits into a small hole. There is also cherry-pit spitting, something most of us have indulged in at one time or other (well, I have). If you think you are good at it, the world record stands at 29.12 metres.

The traditional game is celebrated by the likeable seventeenth-century poet Robert Herrick of *Gather ye Rosebuds* and *Cherry Ripe* (he liked cherries) fame:

> *Julia and I did lately sit*
> *Playing for sport at cherry-pit:*
> *She threw; I cast; and, having thrown,*
> *I got the pit, and she the stone.*

This rhyme seems innocent enough, if a little impenetrable, but Herrick was a wistful bachelor with other things on his mind; Julia was his muse, and 'pit' and 'stone' coy allusions.

Raspberry *Rubus idaeus*

DESCRIPTION	Cane-like perennial 1–1.5 metres. Leaves pointed oval, serrated edge, finely hairy and light green above, densely hairy and white below. Stems with soft thorns and minute hairs. Flowers like small Blackberry flowers. Fruit smaller than cultivated varieties and often paler
HABITAT	Hedgerows, woods – usually in a clearing
DISTRIBUTION	Throughout the British Isles, except the Fens
SEASON	Late June–late August

There aren't many wild foods I am as pleased to see as the wild Raspberry. I know half a dozen locations where it grows and I am always on the lookout for more. Fortunately, I seldom need to worry about competition from other foragers – until the berries redden most people pass them by as slightly odd-looking brambles.

The Raspberry is a native of the British Isles, although there has been some naturalisation of cultivated strains. Their old name was Raspis or Raspis-berry, from a French sweet rose-coloured wine called *Raspise*. A common alternative name was Hindberry and, less common, Mount Ida Bramble – from Pliny's description of it on the mountain in Crete and reflected in its Latin name.

The fruit is exactly the same as the garden variety, save being a little smaller, so needs neither introduction nor warning of deadly look-alikes. The Raspberry is a perennial, with the berries growing on last year's canes. Even before the berries arrive it is easily distinguished from Blackberry by the very soft thorns and pale leaves. Broadleaf woodland clearings are by far the best place to find them, sometimes in abundance. I know of one clearing that contains half an acre of Raspberries, though exactly where is the sort of information I impart only to my direct descendants. Sadly wild Raspberry canes are not as burdened with fruit as the Blackberry and you will have to work hard to collect a good amount. They are not that easy to pick either. Less than perfectly ripe, they cling on until you squash them with pulling and the moment you touch the ripe ones they drop off to disappear frustratingly into the undergrowth. Do not take children with you to pick them – they will eat them all.

Raspberries do not keep well so deal with them as soon as you get home. There are many recipes for Raspberries but only one which does justice to the wild variety - eat them raw with a little caster sugar. If you find more than you can eat you should just try harder to eat them; failing that you could make Raspberry vinegar or retain their beauty by using them on a cheesecake.

Dewberry

Also look out for the Dewberry (*Rubus caesius*). The humble Dewberry has tendency to look like a failed Blackberry. The individual druplets are larger, fewer dusty-looking and irregular in size. It does, however, taste very good, being consistently sharper in flavour than a Blackberry. The plant is low and rather rambling, and grows in damp woods, along grassy paths and scrubland. Like the Raspberry, its thorns are relatively soft. The main problem with the Dewberry is picking the berries. These are soft, succulent and burst with great ease. Either take the time to be very careful or use a fork to pull the berries away. Alternatively you could take Richard Mabey's advice by snipping them off at the stem with scissors and eating them like cocktail cherries.

P.S. The Raspberry is not a plant that has enjoyed a great medicinal reputation. Even Culpeper, a herbalist who found miracle cures everywhere, says, '*I find no great virtue in the leaves.*' There does persist, however, the belief that a tea (or, heaven help us, a pessary) made from the leaves stimulates the uterus during (and after) childbirth. A grim account from the nineteenth century details a meddling intervention in delivering an afterbirth which would no doubt have made an appearance when it was good and ready. The story in St Mark's Gospel of the woman who '*had suffered many things of many doctors, and had spent all she had, and was nothing bettered, but rather grew worse*' is peculiarly relevant here. Modern science has not found any unequivocal medicinal effect for Raspberry leaves so there probably isn't one.

Dog Rose *Rosa canina*

DESCRIPTION	Long arching shrub to 2.5 metres. Leaves oval/pointed, serrated edge. Stems woody, green when young, with strong, sharp red thorns. Flowers usually pink, sometimes white. Hips red, pointed oval
HABITAT	Hedgerow and scrub
DISTRIBUTION	Very common throughout the British Isles
SEASON	Petals May–July, hips from August

Field Rose *Rosa arvensis*

DESCRIPTION	Trailing plant to 1.5 metres. Leaves oval/pointed, serrated edge. Stems woody, green when young, with curved thorns and wiry hairs. Flowers always white, styles forming a *central column*. Hips red, smaller and rounder than those of the Dog Rose
HABITAT	Hedgerow, wood and scrub
DISTRIBUTION	Very common south of the Humber, rare elsewhere
SEASON	Petals June–August, hips from August

These roses are delicate and modest affairs of white and pink – a far cry from the brash cultivars that fill our gardens. Yet there is much joy to be had from our native roses. If we include the many hybrids, there are around a hundred roses to be found wild or naturalised in the British Isles. Of these, fourteen are native and only the two mentioned above are really common.

Anyone who has walked along a country lane in June will not have failed to notice the lovely blossoms of the Dog Rose – it is a constant and familiar part of a British summer. The petals are edible in jams and jellies, but their slight fragrance is easily lost in cooking and the best way to use them is scattered on a summer salad. The white petals of the straggling Field Rose are even less fragrant and lack the pretty pink of its cousin. A tea can be made from the leaves, if you like that sort of thing.

With both these species, however, the real value comes from the hips. These can be gathered from August until November, though I have often found them hanging on past Christmas. The flavour varies a great deal with ripeness and whether or not

Dog Rose

Field Rose

Japanese Rose

Rosehips

they have endured a frost, but I will collect them as long as they look reasonably healthy. The uncompromising thorns make picking them hazardous work and you will need to take things slowly, with gloves and scissors a must.

The taste of Rosehip Syrup is imprinted pleasantly on my mind from the bottles of the stuff my mother gave me as a child. (The memory is not entirely unsullied by dark thoughts, however, because the spoonful of syrup was always preceded by a spoonful of cod-liver oil.) The syrup is fruity and not quite like anything else.

The hips are an extension of the stem and not actually the fruit – the real fruits are inside, covered in hairs. These hairs can be quite a serious irritant so if you wish to make a syrup, or anything else, they must be removed. This can be done by the messy and time-devouring process of splitting the hips open and taking them out. This way the flesh is preserved more or less intact, not reduced to a juice or purée, and can be used in such historical delicacies as Rosehip tart.

More sensible, however, is to cook the hips whole in water, occasionally and gently mashing them with a potato masher after they have softened and continuing to simmer for a total of 15 minutes. The juice is squeezed through a double layer of muslin, the muslin is then cleaned and the juice passed through again.

If you want to make Rosehip Syrup, use 250ml water for every 150g of hips. Put the finished juice in a pan with 150g granulated sugar and stir over a low heat until dissolved, then bring to the boil and take off the heat. This is fairly low in sugar so should be used quite quickly and kept in the fridge, but it will keep for longer if poured hot into hot sterilised jars and sealed with a lid – as you would a jam.

Rosehip Syrup is the basis for nearly everything that can be made from hips – ice cream, sorbet, ice lollies – it is even used to flavour cakes and biscuits. I use it with a vanilla panna cotta, on pancakes and for Rosehip Babas with Blackberries (p.224). You can, of course, just eat it by the spoonful – it contains a lot of vitamin C and is terribly good for you – with or without the cod-liver oil.

Also look out for the Japanese Rose (*R. rugosa*). This plant is an enthusiastic immigrant, common in gardens, but also in hedgerows, roadsides and on sand dunes by the sea, often becoming the dominant plant wherever it finds a home. The flowers are a deep pink, of medium size and intensely perfumed. In addition it has, like my Auntie Hilda from Lowestoft, enormous hips. Unlike most other roses, the hips and flowers are often on the bush at the same time. Being so large, the hips are a shortcut to making Rosehip Syrup, but not one as good as that made from our own roses. It is scattered throughout the British Isles, with a distinct coastal preference.

Our native roses can have a lovely perfume, but it is faint and fleeting. The Japanese Rose, however, is breathtakingly fragrant and the one to use in Turkish Delight (p.232) and in the glorious Rose Jelly (p.242). Nor need you stint on your main ingredient since, being an invader, the Japanese Rose can be picked freely.

Wild Strawberry *Fragaria vesca*

DESCRIPTION	Low, straggling perennial. Leaves trefoil, leaflets pointed/oval, sharply toothed edge, grooved, shiny, green/yellow. Long runners. Flowers five-petalled, 12–18mm diameter, white. Fruit about 1cm diameter
HABITAT	Dry grassy places, woodland clearings, hedgerow, old gardens, waste ground, old railway lines
DISTRIBUTION	Common throughout the British Isles, though rare in the extreme north of Scotland
SEASON	June–August, but may continue to autumn

'*Doubtless God could have made a better berry, but doubtless God never did.*' So the writer Dr William Butler inarguably asserted in the seventeenth century.

The tiny Wild Strawberry that we find in the hedges and woods is not an escapee from our gardens, reverted to its wild form, but a genuine native plant. In fact the cultivated strawberry that we know today did not originate with our own Wild Strawberry. It is a cross between two species from the Americas – the large but tasteless Chilean strawberry, *F. chiloensis,* and the small but flavoursome Virginian strawberry, *F. virginiana*. This garden strawberry was first bred in the mid-eighteenth century, but both prior to this and for some time after, the wild native was brought into gardens and tended with appropriate care. The Alpine strawberries one sees at garden centres and in seed catalogues are mostly cultivars of the native species, thus continuing this practice.

Although a common species, the Wild Strawberry does not appear in abundance everywhere and you really need to find your patch in order to gather them in any quantity. A good spot, such as a recently felled woodland clearing, can provide a red carpet of berries. My best place is a disused railway embankment where the poor, thin, dry soil and the open light provide the perfect habitat. Even where they grow in huge numbers, Wild Strawberries are not the easiest of fruits to pick. They are, of course, very small – their Latin name, *Fragaria vesca*, means 'the small fragrant one' – and they crush easily. Use a shallow basket or box, preferably with a tea-towel in the bottom to protect your prize. This, of course, assumes that you will be taking them home; just remember that such an action may result in sharing them with people who will be grateful but never quite grateful enough.

Wild Strawberries have a long fruiting season – in exceptional years you can start picking in early June and continue until October. The food writer Jane Grigson talks of brushing away some snow one winter to find a good quantity of Wild

Strawberries lying beneath, though it is possible that these were yet another species, the occasionally cultivated, hardy and delicious Hautbois strawberry, *F. moschata*.

Wild Strawberries are time-consuming delicacies to pick and seldom come by the bucketful. It is therefore wise to use your precious find carefully – jams, pies and wines, sadly, are off the menu. I favour keeping the berries whole and visible, preserving their flavour, beauty and texture – a decoration on a cheesecake or fruit flan, preserved in brandy and sugar (p.239), or eaten simply with cream.

P.S. Talking of Strawberries and cream, Robert Herrick, who wrote so naughtily about Cherries (see p.84), writes about them again but, being a bit of a soft-fruit fan, this time includes Strawberries in his verse. For the sake of decency, I have omitted the second half of the poem and the title – you'll just have to look it up.

> *Have ye beheld, with much delight,*
> *A red-Rose peeping through a white?*
> *Or else a Cherrie, double grac't,*
> *Within a Lillie? Center plac't?*
> *Or ever mark't the pretty beam,*
> *A Strawberry shows halfe drown'd in Creame?*

Gooseberry *Ribes uva-crispa*

DESCRIPTION	Shrub 1–2 metres tall. Leaves broad, lobed, dark green, finely hairy. Branches spiny. Fruit green with pale striations taking on a reddish hue with maturity, dried petals persisting at the end
HABITAT	Hedgerow, wood margins, river gorges, areas of previous habitation
DISTRIBUTION	Fairly common throughout the British Isles, except for mountainous and high hill country, and the Fens
SEASON	Late May until July

Having managed to lose a Gooseberry up my nose at the age of four (a story of which my mother has not tired in over half a century), I have always had an intimate relationship with this most comforting denizen of the school dinner hall. There is something very British about the understated Gooseberry. It is indeed a native plant, preferring our damp and mild climate – and its finer points seem more appreciated here than anywhere else.

Wild Gooseberry bushes are found only occasionally, so do keep a lookout for them on your country walks and make a mental note of any you encounter, especially in the spring when the bush will advertise its existence by showing green before most of its neighbours. Even should you find one, disappointment may still be yours as they do not always fruit and that bane of the hedgerow harvester – the farm hedge-trimmer – may devastate in seconds any crop that does appear.

If you have negotiated these problems then you have a great prize. The wild form is inevitably smaller than its many cultivated cousins, though the welcome garden escapees that are often found in the hedgerow may be larger. As with the cultivated Gooseberry, the later the fruit is picked the sweeter it becomes, except that the later you pick it the more likely it is that some other forager (may he or she rot in hell) has helped themselves.

Cooking with Gooseberries is a straightforward matter. The really sweet ones can be eaten raw, though these are rare in the wild variety. Sauce and chutney, jam and jelly, sorbet and fool, pudding and pie, cake and crumble – all wonderful and simple foods, though they can be improved. There is another hedgerow favourite which complements the Gooseberry perfectly – the Elderflower. If you ever try Gooseberry and Elderflower fool then you will never go back to plain Gooseberry.

Redcurrant *Ribes rubrum*

DESCRIPTION	Shrub 1–1.5 metres tall. Stems erect. Leaves maple-like, mostly hairless. Flowers tiny, five-petalled, pink. Bright-red berries, hanging down
HABITAT	Hedgerows, shady woods, overhanging river banks
DISTRIBUTION	Common in England, more so in the South; central Northern Ireland, central and northeast Scotland
SEASON	Flowers April–May. Berries June–July

I have a fondness for the humble Redcurrant which can only be regarded as a triumph of optimistic anticipation over experience. In spring its frothy pink flowers can fill the hedgerows and woodland clearings and every year a bumper harvest is promised. Then attrition sets in. Most of the hedgerow blossoms disappear with the attention of the summer hedge-trimmers and most of those that survive refuse to set. The green berries remain stubbornly green for weeks and many either commit suicide and drop off or fall victim to colour-blind chaffinches. A pitiful few red berries develop for the once-hopeful forager and picking a useful amount will involve several hours' work and much travelling.

Nevertheless, it is a common plant so you should have little trouble in finding some. A few plants are clear garden escapees and likely to be better fruited than wild natives. Look out for Redcurrant's distinctive leaves in spring and go back in the summer. My best patch is mixed in with the overhanging trees on a stream edge, but this does mean that harvesting requires wading up and down in wellies.

It would be nice to say that wild Redcurrants are worth the wait and the work, but frankly they are not. They are sharp in flavour but not unpleasant and, while they would look good decorating a cheesecake, most sensible recipes involve straining out the large number of unwelcome pips. Redcurrant jelly is the favourite of course, but the best way to do justice to the few berries you are likely to find is by making a table jelly dessert with another summer fruit such as Strawberry, Raspberry or Cherry set inside, whole. Simply cook the Redcurrants with a little water, strain, add sugar to taste and some soaked leaf gelatine (about 5g for every 250ml of liquid). Heat through until the gelatine has dissolved, then cool for 10 minutes. Scatter the fresh wild fruit in a glass bowl, pour the liquid redcurrant jelly over and refrigerate to set.

If the berries prove too much work there is Redcurrant leaf tea. It is one of the best of the hedgerow drinks, but tea made from the flowers is even better. I will confess to being a bit of a builder where herbal tea is concerned, but that made from Redcurrant blossom is superb – it tastes like tea.

Fennel *Foeniculum vulgare*

DESCRIPTION	Tall, upright, branched perennial, 1–2.5 metres. Leaves exceedingly fine and feathery, grey/green. Flowers in a yellow umbrella spray. Seeds with black edge. All parts smell strongly of aniseed
HABITAT	Near habitation, waste ground, coastal
DISTRIBUTION	Fairly common in southern England, scarce in the North and Scotland, coastal in Wales. Absent from Ireland
SEASON	Spring until summer for the leaves, late summer and autumn for the seeds

Fennel is not a native of these islands and it still seems a little unsure of itself even after two thousand years, preferring odd corners of the urban environment and seaside car parks to any pristine wilderness. It probably just likes the milder climate such places afford. Fennel is in fact a Mediterranean plant and probably one of the things the Romans did for us. The ancient Greek name for it is *Maratha*, after the city-state of Marathon, where it grew in profusion before it all got trampled to death by runners.

There will never be any problem in identifying this plant because of the unusually fine, feathery leaves and the distinctive aniseed smell. The leaves can appear as early as December in sheltered spots, though March is more typical, and will continue until the summer. The plants can be enormous and usually come in little colonies, so there will be plenty to gather – you often see Fennel in expensive and tiny packets in supermarkets and it is more than usually rewarding to pick it for nothing. It is one of the safest urban plants to collect because its height puts it out of reach of all but the tallest and most talented of dogs.

In late summer and autumn a second crop appears – the seeds. These are tiny compared to the commercially grown ones, but just as good to eat. They will need to be collected just before, or just as they ripen.

Finally, one more crop can be obtained – a diminished and slightly tough form of Florence Fennel from the swollen stem bases. This is best collected in spring as the young shoots appear. The problem with this, of course, is that you will destroy the whole plant and have nothing for next year.

The main use for Fennel is as an accompaniment to fish. This felicitous association goes back to antiquity. For some reason, maybe for pious fear of the sin of gluttony, relatively few recipes survive from earlier times; nearly all references to what we

consider to be foodstuffs are to their medical application, not their culinary ones. Nevertheless, some were written down and survive to this day. Here is a surprisingly modern-sounding one from *The Cook's and Confectioner's Dictionary* of 1723:

> *Gut and wash your Mackerel, then either slit or gash them down the Back, that they may take the Seasoning, then lay them a while in Oil, Salt, Pepper and Fennel; then wrap them up in the Fennel, lay them upon a Gridiron, and broil them. Make a Sauce for them, of clarified Butter, sweet Herbs shred small, Salt, Nutmeg, Gooseberries, Fennel, a little Vinegar and Capers.*

Quite why Fennel works so well with fish I do not know. Culpeper, determined to find the explanation for all things in the heavens, suggests that it is '*because it is a herb of Mercury, and under Virgo, and therefore bears antipathy to Pisces*'.

Pork also benefits from the addition of Fennel leaves or seeds, and of course the leaves can simply be added to any salad. My most unusual success was a home-grown anise made by adding a dessertspoonful of the seeds to a bottle of white rum, which takes on the sweet anise flavour almost immediately.

Ground Elder *Aegopodium podagraria*

DESCRIPTION	Creeping, medium perennial, to 30–60cm. Leaves compound, up to nine leaflets with pointed/oval or irregular serrated edge. Young leaflets bright, shiny, yellowish. Flowers white, umbrella-shaped spray
HABITAT	Gardens, woods, hedgerow. Most often near habitation
DISTRIBUTION	Very common throughout the British Isles, except the north of Scotland
SEASON	March and through until October if you keep cutting it back

I think it is fair to say that Ground Elder is not a popular plant. It was introduced to these islands at some point lost to history by a person who would sap our strength and will. Quite why certain plants have the ability to survive everything nature and human ingenuity can throw at them, while others give up the ghost even when lavished with love, is a mystery.

We have 'tomato blight' and 'pea root rot' but never 'Ground Elder wilt' or 'bindweed botrytis', or if we do they are not doing their jobs properly. The only gardening I am prepared to engage in is the careful removal of Ground Elder from a much-loved lily of the valley patch. It takes an hour of back-breaking work and has to be repeated three times a year. The weed even grows in my lawn and not even grass likes growing there.

Yet this pernicious plant has one saving grace – it is edible. This usefulness in the kitchen is why, of course, Ground Elder was introduced to the British Isles, not malign intent. No doubt the first person to plant it here was delighted to see how well it liked its new home, but as it grew out of favour it continued to grow in the garden regardless.

In the Middle Ages Ground Elder was used extensively as a (totally ineffective) remedy for gout – even carrying some around was believed to be efficacious. This is testified by one of the plant's names – Goutweed – and also by the second part of its Latin name, *podagra* meaning 'gout'. It was also known by the similar Goatweed, though this may be a reference to the shape of the leaves, and indeed the first part of the Latin name means 'goat's foot'. The common name arises because the leaves and flowers are similar to those of the unrelated Elder tree.

Ground Elder is clearly a plant you will have no trouble finding; if you are lucky enough *not* to have any in your garden you will be a welcome visitor at the house of anyone who *does* have it in theirs. Failing this, it can be found easily in woods and hedgerows, especially near habitation. Although Ground Elder is a member of the dangerous carrot family, along with the deadly Hemlocks, it is an easy plant to identify. The leaves are unusually broad and lacking in deeply incised edges. The new shoots, with their folded, shiny yellow-green leaves, appear as early as March and these are by far the best ones to collect. The leaves are, however, edible up until the stage when the plant flowers, at which point their chemistry changes somewhat and they become tough, odd in flavour and slightly laxative. Continual picking and cutting back will ensure renewed growth until the autumn, so there will be a constant supply.

The flavour of the very young leaves is indistinguishable from a good parsley, but more succulent, so it is as a garnish, like parsley, that I normally use it. The leaves can also be cooked as a vegetable like a (slightly stringy) parsley-flavoured spinach and served with butter. I have made Ground Elder soup and Ground Elder quiche, all the tastier for being made from the bodies of an enemy. If you keep guinea pigs it is well worth feeding them with as much Ground Elder as you can – it gives a lovely fresh flavour to the meat.

Hogweed *Heracleum sphondylium*

DESCRIPTION	Tall, robust biennial/perennial to 2 metres. Leaves broad, deeply divided, bristly. Stem bristly, green or dull red. Flowers in umbrella sprays, greyish white
HABITAT	Roadsides, field edges, waste ground
DISTRIBUTION	Very common throughout the UK, except the north of Scotland
SEASON	March–June, though often available later

This rather furry-looking plant does not appear particularly appetising, yet its young shoots are one of the best hedgerow treasures. Once the leaves have opened they lose much of their charm, though. As the various names – Hogweed, Pig's Parsnip and Pigweed – suggest, they have long been fed to pigs. Hogweed has also been called Cow Parsnip and it was no doubt a general fodder plant.

You will have no trouble finding Hogweed – barely a roadside or field edge in the country is bereft of it. While it is an easy plant to recognise, it does belong to the notorious carrot family and you will need to take care. The famous Giant Hogweed is also superficially similar, but produces a sap which causes dermatitis on exposure to sunlight. Most botanicals tell us that the two plants are easy to tell apart as one is seldom more than 1.5 metres tall, while the other reaches 4 metres or more, but as it is the young shoots that are eaten, this distinction is of little help. Normally, however, last year's dry flower stems will persist from both plants and if any are 4 metres tall you will have an excellent clue. In addition, the leaflets of Giant Hogweed are more pointed and are softly hairy on the underside, while its stems are a blotchy red.

Normally you will cut the individual young Hogweed shoots from a plant that is less than half a metre high, slicing with a knife as low down as you can. The younger they are and the less formed the leaf, the better they will taste. The root has plenty of food in store and will continue to send up young shoots for a couple of months or more, making Hogweed a genuine 'cut-and-come-again' plant. Some of the shoots are particularly fat. These are the sheathed flower shoots and, when very young, are even tastier than those of the leaves.

The flavour of cooked Hogweed shoots is frequently likened to asparagus. Well, they are certainly succulent, retaining little of the fibrous texture of the raw shoot, but the taste is nearer parsley than asparagus. The longer they are cooked, the less of the parsley flavour remains and the sweeter (and unfortunately, soggier) they become. They can be steamed and eaten with butter and black pepper, but the best way to serve them is dipped as Hogweed Tempura (p.202).

Pignut *Conopodium majus*

DESCRIPTION	Small upright perennial. Height around 30cm. Basal leaves fine and fern-like, later leaves forming delicate fronds from the stem joints. Flower heads white and umbrella-shaped. Tuberous root, irregular, rounded, up to 25mm diameter at the end of a long, fine root thread
HABITAT	Hedgerow banks, woods, old pasture. Prefers dry soil
DISTRIBUTION	Common all over the UK, except for the Fens
SEASON	All year, but tubers can only be found easily from February to July when the plant is visible

The hunt for the Pignut is like no other – something between a search, a puzzle and a test of dexterity. The 'nut' (really it is a tuber, like its relative, the carrot) cannot just be dug up, it must be searched out by following the infuriatingly delicate root fibre down, and north a bit then maybe southeast until the prize is located. Break the fibre and all is lost. The feeling of triumph at locating the tiny reward is a great foraging moment. On one of the wild-food forays I lead, hard-hearted stockbrokers were on their hands and knees begging for time to find just one more Pignut.

To find the nut you must first learn the plant. The feather-like fronds of the young plant are fairly distinctive, though Fool's Parsley is not too dissimilar and may cause confusion. Fool's Parsley tends to grow as a weed of cultivation – vegetable gardens being its preferred habitat. It has more substantial leaves, the flower heads have conspicuous long, thin spikes projecting from underneath them and – even if you are still fooled – there is no nut to find. Pignuts nearly always grow in fairly large groups so you may find yourself in one place for a long time. I know a field in Devon that seems to grow little else. As you need to dig up the nuts, permission will be required if it is not on your own land. Since their frequent habitat is old wildlife-rich pasture you should be careful not to disturb the turf too much – dig up a few here and a few there and do it as carefully as you can. Although the nuts are available all year they are only findable when the plant is visible – from February to July. It seems likely that Pignuts are the heroes of the otherwise inexplicable rhyme 'Here we go gathering nuts in May'.

Pursuit of this earthy treasure has long been a children's pastime, but I know of none that enjoy it now, even in my rural village. It's a pity that such a simple pleasure has been lost. Pignuts have not found much of a place in the primitive medicine cabinet though Culpeper tells us that being a plant under Venus '… *they provoke lust exceedingly, and stir up those sports she is mistress of…*'. You have been warned.

Are they worth all that effort to find? If you were planning a wild dinner party, Pignuts would not form more than a tiny part of the meal. Collecting enough for any more would be the work of several days. As an occasional treat, though, they are highly recommended. Uncooked the flavour is faintly sweet and similar to a Hazelnut. Cooked it is more like Sweet Chestnut. They take a bit of cleaning, though there is no pressing reason to peel off the thin brown skin. They can be added raw to salads or cooked in stews. Sliced and toasted in a little oil, they are excellent added to a stir-fry or a Wild Garlic Pesto (p.205). Of course you can just sit in the grass for an hour, digging, scrubbing, nibbling and meditating.

P.S. The existence of Pignuts in a location is a good sign of its biodiversity. Unfortunately, this is something of a two-edged sword. Pignuts were not given their name for nothing as pigs, which can smell them from some distance, will go to great lengths to dig them up. Wild boar have long been extinct in these islands but have made an inadvertent comeback as farm escapees – either accidentally or as part of an ill-advised blow for animal rights – and are now breeding in southwest England and elsewhere. The snout of the wild boar is a formidable instrument, able to overturn large areas of turf in search of this favourite food. I have seen hundreds of acres of downland – previously rich in flowers, fungi and invertebrates – ploughed up by these animals looking for a tasty morsel. This assault obviously damages all that grows there, but it also releases nitrogen which encourages coarse grasses to grow and inhibits recovery. Maybe we ought to eat all the Pignuts we can after all.

Young Pignut with early spring leaves

Sweet Cicely *Myrrhis odorata*

DESCRIPTION	Medium tall perennial, to 1.5 metres. Leaves fern-like. Stems hollow, hairy. Large tap root. Seed pods vertical, ribbed and long. Flowers in white umbrella. All parts smell of aniseed
HABITAT	Hedgerows, wood margins, often near water
DISTRIBUTION	Common, but with a northern distribution. England north of a line from Birmingham to Scarborough, Scottish lowlands and east-central Northern Ireland. Sparse in Wales
SEASON	Leaves from March until October, best early. Seed pods in June and July. Roots in October

As a confirmed southerner this is a plant I seldom get to see, yet in the North it can fill the roadside much as Cow Parsley does in the South. Superficially the two hedgerow scenes look the same, but they certainly don't taste the same and I envy my northern friends their good fortune. Sweet Cicely's distribution is rather odd, but its frequent appearance near habitation suggests it was introduced, then became naturalised in the cooler North where the climate was more like its mountainous central European home.

It is not a hard plant to identify but it *is* a member of the notorious carrot family and care must be exercised, especially if you intend to eat the root. The easy test is to rub the leaves and sniff. If you smell aniseed you are probably on the right track, with only the equally edible Fennel smelling the same. The 'sweet' part of the name is well deserved – the chemical which provides the aniseed flavour is a sweetener too. It has also been called Sweet Chervil and even the rather nice Candy Carrot.

The uses of Sweet Cicely are endless and some employ the sweetness to advantage – the leaves can be sprinkled on trifles or strawberries, or used as an additional sweetener for rhubarb. They can be included in a salad, of course, but also in place of Fennel in any number of dishes, fishy ones being the most obvious. The young and strongly aromatic pods are eaten too, sometimes as an on-the-go snack, and the roots may be sliced in a salad, roasted or boiled or even, as suggested by the herbalists, candied to protect against the plague.

Finally, the last two wicked lines of an eighteenth-century poem:

Sing, sweet Cicely, sing no more,
Till Love be deaf, as well as blind.

Wild Parsnip *Pastinaca sativa*

DESCRIPTION	Medium/tall biennial, to 1.5 metres. Pinnate leaflets opposite, irregularly lobed, toothed, hairy. Stem ribbed, hairy. Flowers in yellow umbrella sprays
HABITAT	Bare places, roadsides, sand dunes
DISTRIBUTION	Complex distribution. Southeast of a line from the Humber to the Severn, though rare in north Devon and Cornwall. Frequent in South Wales, locally common in coastal northern England. Scarce elsewhere
SEASON	Roots in the autumn

Wild Parsnips are the same species as garden parsnips and their complex distribution suggests that much of the wild population has returned to the wild after a domestic sojourn. Although the fully grown plants look vigorous enough, the only bit we eat – the roots – are pathetic affairs compared to the giants we are used to. Nevertheless, they taste splendidly of parsnip.

The roots are best dug in the autumn, but by then most of the plant will be skeletal and will have lost many identifying features. The best thing is to get to know your plants and observe the older members of the population develop their distinctive yellow flowers before they die back. This will help you avoid confusion with several poisonous members of the carrot family, such as the Hemlocks. Parsnips are, of course, biennials and the plants you will be digging up are those that have completed one season's growth. Parsnip is rather like its relative the Giant Hogweed in that contact with it can sensitise the skin to sunlight and cause dermatitis. It is by no means as dangerous in this respect, but it may be worth using gloves to be safe.

There is really only one way of cooking Wild Parsnips which will do justice to the small amount you are likely to find – parsnip crisps. Just slice them thinly and deep-fry in a good cooking oil until they are, well, crisp.

Also look out for the Wild Carrot (*Daucus carota*). This is the ancestor of the cultivated carrot, which now possesses subspecies status as *Daucus carota sativus*. As with the Wild Parsnip, you are not going to be able to replace your home-grown or bought-in crop with the wild ancestor, but it is common enough to try out occasionally. It has a similar southeastern distribution to the Wild Parsnip, but with a distinctly maritime preference, though this is quite likely to be another subspecies – *gummifer*. At no more than 70cm, it is a fairly low plant, with typical feathery leaves and dense white/grey flower heads with conspicuous bracts growing out from the edge. The root is, again, rather a disappointment, but it does look like a carrot (except for its colour, which is pale) and taste like a carrot.

Both these plants are included for their interest more than their genuine usefulness in the kitchen. The fact that they must be dug up argues against their extensive collection because of the collateral damage that is caused and permissions that must be obtained. Frankly I do not expect many will try them more than once or twice – conservation and legal worries aside, they are too much like hard work.

Wild Parsnip

Common Sorrel *Rumex acetosa*

DESCRIPTION	Upright, medium perennial. 30–100cm tall. Basal leaves forming a rosette, arrow-shaped with sharply pointed lobes. Higher leaves clasping stem. Mature leaves reddening. Single stem, seldom branched, reddening. Flower spike tall, flowers and seeds rusty pink. All parts taste acidic
HABITAT	Rough pasture, hedgerow, woods. Prefers neutral to acid soils
DISTRIBUTION	Very common everywhere
SEASON	It is often possible to find some all year but the spring and the second growth in the autumn are best

Sorrel is a very close relative of the dozen or so docks that live in these islands. They are all members of the Polygonaceae, a family which includes other familiar plants such as bistort, redshank, buckwheat and Japanese knotweed. Most familiar of all is rhubarb with which Sorrel shares its fruity flavour. Sorrel has long been used as a food and also as a medicine, most usually for its cooling properties.

You will have no trouble finding Sorrel – almost any field and hedgerow will sport some, although it is less common on chalk. The mature plants are highly conspicuous in summer with their rusty pink flower spikes, which slowly turn red brown as the seeds mature. These tall plants of late spring and summer provide little in the way of fresh leaves, but from February the bright new rosettes appear from the perennial root and a second growth follows in late summer through to early winter.

Identification is not difficult though the docks may distract you for a moment. The most worrying look-alike is the poisonous Lords and Ladies (*Arum maculatum*, p.191). This is a vastly different plant but the leaves are superficially similar and sometimes almost identical (as the picture on p.193 shows). On a recent walk a friend accidentally picked Lords and Ladies leaves and put them in my basket thinking they were giving me a present of Sorrel. This, at least, is my charitable assessment of the incident. There are two ways to be sure – Lords and Ladies leaves are relatively thin compared to the rather succulent leaves of Sorrel and its backward-pointing lobes are always *rounded* whereas those of Sorrel are sharply *pointed*. Do not use the taste test here unless you want your tongue and lips to go numb and swell up.

Sorrel is often added to a salad of milder leaves as it is a little too strong on its own. More often it is used to make a sauce, for example with yogurt, the shredded leaves being sweated for a couple of minutes, then for a minute or two longer in the

yogurt. Alternatively, you can just mix the shredded leaves in raw. Fish dishes are the most obvious targets for Sorrel sauce, but meats such as veal, chicken and pork benefit too. Sorrel's capabilities do not stop there. It makes a terrific omelette – either straight into the mix or as a creamy sauce inside – and it can even be used to provide acidity to puddings.

The taste of Sorrel comes from oxalic acid and calcium oxalate. These are quite seriously poisonous and in a sufficiently reckless dose will cause vomiting, muscular twitching, convulsions, renal failure, cardiac arrest and even milk-fever (though I think you need to be a cow for the last one). Oxalic acid removes calcium from the bloodstream, turning it into calcium oxalate (from which you can make your very own kidney stones) and resulting in hypocalcaemia. There is at least one recorded occasion in which a fatality occurred due to eating Sorrel; it was in Spain. One serving of the guilty soup contained a substantial (though not *that* substantial) half kilogram of the plant and the unfortunate victim was not at all in the best of health even before his final meal. As long as you are reasonably fit a small amount of Sorrel will do you no harm, just don't eat it by the bucketful.

Also look out for Sheep's Sorrel (*Rumex acetosella*), a smaller but very similar plant. The key difference is the lobes on the leaves which are more like wings, or halberd-shaped as they are often described. It is strictly a lover of acid soils.

Stinging Nettle *Urtica dioica*

DESCRIPTION	Upright perennial, to 1.5 metres. Leaves heart-shaped, opposite on stem, serrated edge, covered in stinging hairs. Stems tough and fibrous, also with stinging hairs
HABITAT	Woods, waste ground, hedgerow, near habitation
DISTRIBUTION	Throughout the UK
SEASON	Spring – before the flowers form, though the younger the better. New growth will appear in summer and autumn from cut-back plants

Revered and reviled but ignored only at a cost, the Stinging Nettle is among the best known of our plants. Indeed it is often the first one we learn, as the splendidly named Reverend Tipping Silvester wrote in 1733:

> *There grows the Product of a scatter'd Seed,*
> *The Nettle, Plant ignoble, baleful Weed.*

Despite its familiarity and long history of use in the kitchen and sickroom, it is shamefully under-exploited these days. Everyone has heard of Nettle Soup but few have ever made it.

Any plant with such overt potency as the Stinging Nettle was likely to accumulate a large number of putative cures to its name. Culpeper lists nearly thirty diseases for which it is the answer and, bringing us up to date, Piers Warren, in his book *101 Uses for Stinging Nettles*, has forty-seven. (Incidentally, don't try the 'X-rated' number '101', it isn't nice… or safe). A few of these remedies make some sense. Stinging Nettles contain vitamin C, so will prevent scurvy, and the substantial levels of iron will alleviate some types of anaemia. In the roots there are antihistamines, making them a likely palliative in hay fever and other allergies. The one disease for which they show most promise went unnoticed by the old herbalists – enlargement of the prostate. One more complaint which Stinging Nettles, used as a poultice, are reputed to cure is haemorrhoids. Just remember to boil them before applying.

I will not need to tell you where to find a supply of Stinging Nettles – few plants are more ubiquitous – and while there are look-alikes in the dead nettles and yellow archangel these are equally edible. Picking Stinging Nettles is always going to be a trial – even with decent gloves. The long stems whip around and invariably get you somewhere. The brave, or foolhardy, can pick them without gloves by moving their fingers upwards and grasping the stem just below the young half-dozen or so leaves at the top. This manoeuvre, which can take a fair amount of painful practice, breaks

the hollow silica hairs from the side so that they do not penetrate the skin. The stinging toxin was long thought to be formic acid – the poison produced by ants – but modern analysis has revealed a cocktail of histamines, acetylcholine, tartaric acid and oxalic acid. Whichever of these is the main culprit, it hurts, and the pain can last a couple of days. The idea of rubbing dock leaves on to the affected area seemingly goes back at least to Chaucer who uses the phrase '*Nettle in Docke out*' in his *Troilus and Criseyde*. Despite its antiquity, it is doubtful if it works and there is also the possibility that it is Common Mallow – formerly known as Round Dock – that the old writers were referring to.

Only young, fresh leaves should be collected. In March the whole plant can be picked, but as they mature, just pick the developing leaves from the top. At the first sign of flowers developing you must stop picking. The plant will now start producing cystoliths – microscopic rods of calcium carbonate – which can be absorbed by the body where they will mechanically interfere with kidney function. By this time the texture and flavour has deteriorated anyway and the plants are not worth picking. Cut-down plants will produce a second fresh growth and it is sometimes possible to pick Stinging Nettles up until November.

Picking them without gloves is one thing but eating them without cooking is quite another. There are some notorious nettle-eating contests held around the country, the best known being at the Bottle Inn in West Dorset. I have never entered this competition but I have eaten raw nettles. The trick is to fold two or three into a large pill first then apply a crushing bite with the molars. It's like eating sandpaper. Beer helps.

A more gentle introduction to nettle consumption is tea. To make one cup, just pour boiling water over half a dozen leaves, steep for 5–10 minutes, then scoop the leaves out. If you like the water left over from boiling Brussels sprouts you'll love it. Of greater interest is Nettle beer. This is more of a sparkling wine than a beer (when I make it anyway) and downing a pint has much the same effect as downing a pint of Champagne.

The flavour of cooked Stinging Nettles is halfway between spinach and a mild cabbage and there is no reason why it cannot be served straight as a vegetable. Thin leaves do not always take well to steaming, so just gently sweat them for 10 minutes in a covered pan with the little bit of water that adheres to the leaves from washing. Serve with some butter and black pepper stirred in. You will be relieved to hear that cooking completely destroys the nettle's ability to sting.

The cooked and coarsely puréed leaves can be dolloped on to a pizza or used to stuff cannelloni. Continuing this distinctly Italian theme, the cooked and finely chopped leaves, squeezed almost dry, are added to flour to make Nettle Ravioli (p.206). Nettles can be used in several of the recipes in this book calling for green leaves but the best of them is the simplest – Nettle Soup (p.201).

Hop *Humulus lupulus*

DESCRIPTION	Long climbing perennial, 2–6 metres. Mature leaves *palmate* (like a hand), edges serrated like a Stinging Nettle. Stems coarsely hairy. Flowers green, male branched sprays, female cone-like, on separate plants
HABITAT	Hedgerow
DISTRIBUTION	Fairly common in England, except for the North and far Southwest. Uncommon in Wales and Scotland, rare in Northern Ireland
SEASON	April and May for the shoots, September for the flowers

The Hop is the only native member of the Cannabaceae family, though I am given to understand that its well-known relative is occasionally and mysteriously seen in remote woodland clearings. While Hops have long been considered a soporific – the Kentish hop-pickers are reputed to have added the Hop resin from their knives to their roll-ups – it is their other recreational use as a flavouring of ale to make beer for which they are famous. In Britain the medicinal and culinary uses of Hops predate their employment in ale. The seventeenth-century writer John Evelyn in his *Discourse of Sallets* considered Hops to be more medicinal than fit for a *sallet* and Culpeper suggests it as a cure for French diseases, whatever they are. Putting the sickroom and bar-room aside, it is the young shoots that are eaten.

The plant disappears to its roots in the winter and cannot be found. In April and May the young shoots trail themselves all over hedges and – provided they do not fall foul of the hedge-trimmer – you should be assured of a good harvest. The leaves are very distinctive with their hand-like shape and serrated edges so you will not risk confusing them with the other trailing hedgerow plants, such as bindweed, or the poisonous Black and White Bryonies (p.195).

While I fancy some of the beeriness comes through in the shoots, the flavour is an unusual one and not easily described – you will just have to try some. They can be enjoyed in a soup, a stir-fry or in pakoras (p.211).

P.S. Hop shoots are the delicacy of but a few and the Hop is best known for its use in beer-making. Hops add not only bitterness and flavour but also stability to a beer. The herbalist Gerard has reassurance for those of us particularly fond of this drink:

The manifold virtues in hops do manifestly argue the holsomnesse of beere above ale; for the hops rather make it phisicall drinke to keepe the body in health, than an ordinarie drinke for the quenching of our thirst.

Young Hop shoots

Before the beneficial properties of Hops were fully appreciated, various other hedgerow plants were used to add bitterness and flavour to ale. The very common and aromatic Mugwort and that denizen of acid peat bogs, Sweet Gale, were two of the most common; Yarrow (p.141), Ground Ivy and the wonderfully named Horehound also found their way into the barrel. Another plant which was employed occasionally is Wormwood (*Artemisia absinthium*). This fairly uncommon plant, famous for its inclusion in another alcoholic drink – absinthe – is one of my favourites due to the heady perfume of its leaves. If you ever find any, just break off a leaf, roll it in your fingers and sniff – it smells like a Turkish tobacconist's.

Watermint *Mentha aquatica*

DESCRIPTION	Medium upright perennial to 80cm, more often 20–30cm. Leaves dark green, pointed/oval, sometimes with a purplish tinge, finely hairy, toothed edge, opposite. Stem square in section, hairy, reddish brown. Flowers lilac, some axial flowers but also a rounded flower head at the top. All parts smell strongly minty
HABITAT	Stream sides, boggy places, damp meadows
DISTRIBUTION	Common throughout the British Isles, except the northern Highlands of Scotland
SEASON	April–November

Even someone as dedicated as I am to not gardening has mint growing by the back door – it is one of those plants that is needed in small quantities just occasionally and has the commendable property of growing vigorously without the slightest effort. Although the particular flavour that the garden varieties supply is hard to find in the wild, there are many native mints to be enjoyed. The most common and most useful of them all is Watermint.

The upright nature, the furry and slightly bronzed leaves and the damp habitat make Watermint an easy plant to spot. Identification is easier than normal as the peppermint-like smell is unmistakable. It is, perhaps, possible to mix it up with another mint, but that is the worst that can happen. Nevertheless remember that this is the preferred home of the deadly Hemlocks so you must be careful.

Watermint is really not hard to find – nestling among the Watercress and Brooklime along a stream edge, or hiding in the reeds and meadowsweet of a wet meadow – but you may need to search a little before you find your spot. When found it is usually in some quantity so you will not have to stint on your recipes. Picking is often an exercise requiring Wellington boots – even if there is a nice patch within reach of the unbooted there is always a nicer one just a little too far away. Scissors are essential tools for collecting this perennial plant – the stems are quite tough and it is all too easy to uproot the whole thing, leaving nothing to grow for next year.

The smell is almost peppermint but not quite. True peppermint is a hybrid of Watermint and Spearmint. Hybrids abound in the mint world, making life difficult for the botanist and interesting for the cook. The smell of Watermint varies from plant to plant and from season to season. The first growth in the spring is the sweetest, with a slight turpentine tone appearing by the autumn. Even the time of

day has some effect – Mary Randolph, writing in 1838 as *The Virginia Housewife*, implores the forager to '*Pick the mint early in the morning while the dew is on it.*'

Many recipes involving the mints require steeping the leaves in a liquid for a period of time. The simplest of these is mint tea. I have always considered a fondness for herbal teas an inexplicable affectation but I tried this and find it less vile than some others. A high recommendation indeed. Back to Mary Randolph, who was picking her mint for a higher purpose, mint cordial, evidently in industrial quantities to see her through the winter.

> *Put two handsful into a pitcher, with a quart of French brandy, cover it, and let it stand till next day; take the mint carefully out, and put in as much more, which must be taken out next day – do this the third time; then put three quarts of water to the brandy, and one pound of loaf sugar powdered; mix it well together – and when perfectly clear, bottle it.*

I highly recommend the recipe for Watermint Sorbet (p.219). It is one of the few desserts that is both delicious and invigorating. Watermint has long been used as a carminative, which is why we still eat mints at the end of the meal (rather ruined when they come in large boxes and are covered in chocolate). As the herbalist Gerard says, '*Mint is marvellous wholesome for the stomacke.*' Watermint *can* be used wherever garden mint is used, but the peppermint flavour may not suit everyone.

P.S. Culpeper has to be quarantined as a p.s. for his comments on mint. Among the many recommendations he has for it is a '*remedy for those that have venereal dreams and pollutions in the night, being outwardly applied*'. How you 'outwardly apply' it he doesn't say. I have given the matter considerable thought and suggest stuffing the leaves in your Y-fronts.

Spearmint *Mentha spicata*

DESCRIPTION	Medium, upright perennial, to 70cm. Leaves distinctly pointed/oval, with neat saw-toothed edge, bright green, almost unstalked, mostly hairless. Stems square in section. Flowers lilac, central spike and some on stalks from the leaf joints. Smells intensely of spearmint!
HABITAT	Roadsides, waste ground. Often a garden escapee
DISTRIBUTION	Frequent throughout the British Isles, but less common in Scotland, Wales and Lincolnshire. Rare in Ireland
SEASON	May–October

Apart from the ubiquitous and delightful Watermint, the most common of all *Mentha* species is Corn Mint (*M. arvensis*). Unfortunately this is not a great asset in any kitchen so I have passed it by; the naturalist and writer Geoffrey Grigson famously describes it as smelling of 'mouldy Gorgonzola'. There are, however, several other, more useful mints which the habitual country rambler is likely to encounter. Perhaps the best of these, certainly the smelliest, is the ancestor of many of our garden varieties, Spearmint.

The flavour of Spearmint needs no introduction but the wild plant will not be familiar to many people. It is, however, one of the easiest of the mints to identify with its ragged-edged, bright-green leaves and, most of all, its toothpaste smell. I know it from several locations, though nowhere near as many as Watermint, and in one of these (a country lay-by) it grows in vast profusion. Spearmint is an introduced species which has become naturalised. For this reason it is often found near habitation.

As with Watermint, Spearmint is best employed in sweet dishes and in drinks, though it has been used in the past – as its garden descendant is today – with lamb.

Also look out for any number of other mints. There are at least a dozen of these if the hybrids are included. The one pictured here is Round-leaved or Apple-scented Mint (*M. suaveolens*), a native species found scattered all over the British Isles but more frequent in the Southwest. It is one of the commonly cultivated species and you are quite likely to find it near habitation.

Spearmint

Round-leaved Mint

Wild Marjoram *Origanum vulgare*

DESCRIPTION	Medium perennial, to 50cm. Leaves pointed/oval, finely and sparsely downy especially the edge, short dark green stalks. Stem thin, reddish brown, square in section. Flowers pink, arising on long stems from the leaf joints. Smell strongly aromatic
HABITAT	Dry grassland, roadsides, scrub. On lime
DISTRIBUTION	Occasional. Scattered throughout the British Isles with a southern bias. Rare in northern Scotland and Northern Ireland
SEASON	May–October

This is the oregano that we find in our pasta sauces and on pizzas; thus we associate it with Italy, yet it is a native species, long appreciated in these islands for its medicinal and culinary properties. The marjoram we typically grow in the garden is one of several related species, such as sweet marjoram (*O. majorana*) and pot marjoram (*O. onites*).

Wild Marjoram is most common in the south of England and it likes chalky soils. As it is a perennial you only have to find it once to have an annual supply. I have a spot – a roadside verge – half a mile from my house where it appears in abundance every year. The six months of the year when it is not producing useful leaves are easily filled as it keeps very well indeed when dried.

The taste is the familiar one – perhaps a little fainter than from plants grown in warmer climates – and it is hardly necessary to describe how it might be deployed. The eighteenth-century food writer Louis Lémery writes: '*Marjoram is an Herb us'd in Sauces, to give your Meat the more Relish*', and it is hard to disagree.

Bilberry *Vaccinium myrtillus*

DESCRIPTION	Short shrub, to 50cm. Leaves oval, 1–3cm, reddening with age, deciduous. Stems green, angled in cross-section. Berries dark blue, almost black, a bloom like a plum, end flattened slightly
HABITAT	Heaths, moors, open woodland – acid soils, never chalk
DISTRIBUTION	Common west of a line drawn from Scarborough to Exeter and scattered on the heaths of south and southeast England
SEASON	August and September

The native Bilberry (or Whortleberry, Blaeberry, Huckleberry or half a dozen other names) is much superior to its North American cousin, the blueberry. But the imported species has one major advantage – you don't have to pick it.

I have spent many, many hours knelt among the huge tracts of Bilberry bushes on Exmoor and Dartmoor with very little to show for my efforts. Although the bushes are common, the berries hang upon them sparsely, and at a back-breaking height. A reasonable rate for handpicking is considered to be 250g per hour. If you are determined to make a better job of collecting your Bilberries then it might be time to invest in a berry-picker (p.13); this is the very best type of berry to use it on but there are the usual disadvantages of damaged berries and unwanted leaves. Peasant children have, in the past, been employed to collect large quantities of Bilberries for market but the less disciplined modern child will most likely come back with nothing more than a smiling purple face and an empty basket.

Largely missing from the rich soils of central and eastern England, this is a berry of wild heath and moor – the picture opposite was taken on a wet and blowy Scottish mountainside. It also grows in open woodland but I have seldom seen berries on these plants, no doubt due to my being out-foraged by deer and ponies.

As you might guess I am one with the child forager when it comes to Bilberries. Not a single Bilberry has ever made it back to my kitchen. But if you are luckier, harder-working or more self-controlled than me, there are wonderful things to be done with half a kilo of Bilberries. The flavour is sharper than the blueberry and richer, but the berries are similarly blessed with a lack of hard pips. Better still, they look wonderful.

I favour recipes that show off the beauty of these berries and speak of the selfless toil that went into their collection. The excellent tart on p.222 does just this but uses the much rarer Cranberry. It would look every bit as good with Bilberries.

Cranberry *Vaccinium oxycoccos*

DESCRIPTION	Slender, low, creeping perennial. Leaves small, sparse, alternate, oval, shiny dark green. Stems thin and straggling. Berries rounded/pear-shaped, red, often mottled
HABITAT	Acid bogs and heaths, open boggy woods. Usually nestled in sphagnum moss
DISTRIBUTION	Uncommon, restricted to wild areas of central and southern Scotland, northwest England, west Wales, central Northern Ireland. Occasional elsewhere. Gather seldom and with care
SEASON	August–October

Fen Berry, Moss Berry, Moor Berry – these names leave us in no doubt where this splendid little plant is to be found. Sadly the Cranberry is much less common and widespread nowadays due to the draining of land for agriculture. It was once found in many parts of southern England but is now almost extinct in this region.

Most of its current strongholds are sensitive and often protected habitats, and even there it is seldom found in abundance. The berries pictured here and on the Cranberry and Apple Tart (p.222) were found on a magnificently grim bog (or 'moss' as it is called) in Galloway after a three-day search during their wettest August week on record. Not exactly easy foraging.

In the eighteenth century, at Longtown on the northern border of Cumberland, 20–30 pounds of Cranberries were sold every day during the five- or six-week season. They were used to make Cranberry tarts. This sort of bounty is not possible today; our commercial Cranberries are all American Cranberries (*Vaccinium macrocarpon*).

Along with Bilberries, Cranberries are a member of the Ericaceae family and are often found nestling in the sphagnum under tufts of heather, itself an ericaceous plant. Finding them is quite a task as the berries are hard to see and the thin plants almost invisible. Once you find a plant there are likely to be more nearby. Do collect with care and restraint, and be careful of the delicate habitat around you.

Cranberries have received a certain amount of attention recently as being half food, half medicine – a 'functional food' as such are called. Its list of nutrients is no more than one would expect from an average fruit, but it does seem to have some ability to ameliorate certain infections, such as those of the urinary tract, by preventing the bacteria from sticking to cells and also a possible benefit in treating cardiovascular disease.

The berries are very beautiful and, while you can make them into sauces and drinks, are best used in a way that shows them in all their rare glory. They are rather sharp and some consider them inedible raw. However, they are certainly not poisonous and if sufficient sugar is used in the recipe the berries will simply add a tart note to the dish – popping in the mouth with a pleasant sharpness if used raw. Like Bilberries, and unlike most other wild berries which can be rather pippy, they contain very small seeds which are hardly noticeable when eaten.

For some reason Cranberries have the longest use-by date of any fruit. I have kept them in an unrefrigerated pot for 3 months with no sign of decay and an eighteenth-century botanical states that '*They may be kept for several years by wiping them clean and closely corking them up in dry bottles.*' Of course, you could just eat them.

Brooklime *Veronica beccabunga*

DESCRIPTION	Low, straggling aquatic perennial, to 60cm. Leaves rounded oval, bright green – paler below, opposite pairs at 90° to each other. Stem hollow, roots issuing from leaf joints part of the way up. Sky-blue, four-petalled flowers
HABITAT	Streams and pond sides, wet paths
DISTRIBUTION	Common throughout the British Isles, except the northwest of Scotland
SEASON	May–November

I am going to be straight with you: Brooklime doesn't taste all that great. This is not a personal opinion – although it is undoubtedly edible, no one I know has a good word to say about it. So why is it here? Four reasons. It *is* edible, it's good for you, it's very common and the Latin name is fun.

Brooklime is a plant found in slow-moving streams and sometimes along wet footpaths. The bright-green leaves are very neat and do look rather tasty. It is just that they aren't. Mixed with other salad ingredients such as Watercress (with which it often grows) and dressed with oil and vinegar, Brooklime is really not bad – this is how it is eaten in mainland northern Europe. Do not even think of cooking it.

Brooklime is one of the speedwells, with the same pretty blue flowers. The leaves are rather rounded, however, and you will not easily confuse it with the other water-loving speedwells. Brooklime suffers the same problems as Watercress regarding liver fluke, so you must read about it (p.47–9) before you embark on a Brooklime salad.

P.S. *Veronica beccabunga* is one of the most remarkable Latin names in existence, which is saying something when you consider it is up against glories such as *Upupa epops* and *Apolysis zzyzxensis*. The name always makes me think of Carmen Miranda. The origin of Veronica is undecided and why it was given to the speedwells obscure. Where *beccabunga* comes from is also uncertain. Most probably it is the German *Bachbunge* meaning 'brook bunch' – the plant does fill up streams with large bunches of itself. Or it could be 'brook bung' – the Norse 'bung' being a reference to it blocking streams, or maybe from the Flemish *beckpunge* meaning 'mouthsmart', a reference to its bitter flavour.

The origin of the common name is also unclear. 'Brook' is straightforward enough, but 'lime' could refer to stream or mud or plant, or the Old English name for speedwell. Nice to get these things sorted out.

Corn Salad *Valerianella locusta*

DESCRIPTION	Low, short, branching annual, to 15cm. Lower leaves spoon-shaped, almost hairless, slightly succulent, opposite. Flowers with five petal-like lobes, tiny, in clusters, pale lilac
HABITAT	Waste ground, agricultural land, gardens
DISTRIBUTION	Frequent in England, increasingly rare in the North. Generally coastal in Wales
SEASON	Late winter and spring

Corn Salad, or Lamb's Lettuce as it is often called, is a mild-flavoured salad plant historically more popular in France than here. The cultivated version, which can be bought from the greengrocer's or grown at home, is larger but even milder. The clusters of tiny pale-lilac flowers make it an easy plant to spot and impossible to mix up with anything nasty. I find it mostly as neat little plants growing in flower beds or on waste ground, but it is also a common weed of agriculture.

It can quickly go to seed so the young growth of winter and spring is the best. I doubt if a salad made entirely from Corn Salad would satisfy many people so it is best used mixed with other, stronger-flavoured leaves and dressed well. The flowers too, are edible and they add a pleasantly powerful fragrance to a salad.

Elder *Sambucus nigra*

DESCRIPTION	Shrub or small tree. Leaves formed from two or three pairs of opposite leaflets plus one terminal leaflet. Leaflets oval and pointed with serrated edge. Flowers in stalked umbrella sprays, five-petalled, cream with yellow stamens. Berries purple/black with three small pips
HABITAT	Hedgerow, disturbed ground near habitation, nitrogen-rich area such as around rabbit warrens
DISTRIBUTION	Very common everywhere, except central and northern Scotland
SEASON	Flowers late May–early July, berries August and September

This untidy weed of a plant has been the source of both comfort and fear for millennia; a tree to both court and counter disaster. Despite its unkempt appearance it is, above all, a plant of power. The superstitions associated with the Elder are legion. To fell the tree is unlucky as it is home to the unforgiving Elder Mother; burning the timber in the house will release the devil within; and to make a cradle from its timber is sheer folly. Yet it has been attributed with innumerable virtues.

Every part, flowers, berries, leaves, bark – and even the soil it grows in and any spring that passes its roots – has been used as a cure for some ailment or other. Warts and sorrows can be transferred to an Elder stick and buried, and an Elder planted near a house (there is one by my back door) will protect the occupants from evil. It will even provide refuge during a thunderstorm as it is, we are told, never struck by lightning. Once you learn of these charming absurdities it is difficult to get them out of your head. I often accidentally break thin branches when collecting flowers or berries and always, without thought or hesitation, say sorry.

How and when the Elder earned its fearful reputation is lost in time but it appears to be pre-Christian. Christianity, however, as it has done so skilfully so often, picked up the pagan tradition and turned it to its own use. The tree from which the remorseful Judas hanged himself was deemed to have been an Elder, and the Cross of Christ was said to have been made from its timber. This association with the Easter story accords perfectly with the ambivalent Elder, for the death of Jesus was, of nature and necessity, both disaster and triumph.

In common with a handful of others species included in this book, the Elder provides two crops, flowers and berries, though there is a third in the Jelly Ear

fungus which grows on the dead branches. There is one novice mistake that I must warn you about. Do not pick all the flowers from a tree, then go back expecting to find some berries. You won't. Find any, that is. Fortunately the Elder is sufficiently common to provide both in great abundance. Its popularity, however, has made some of the more urban and suburban trees the subject of friendly and sometimes not-so-friendly rivalry among springtime cordial and 'Champagne' makers.

The tree is easy to recognise, though a few species such as the related, broader-leaved and earlier-flowering Wayfaring Tree can provide a false dawn for the Elderflower hunter. Later in the year it is even possible to be distracted by the tall umbel of the Hogweed. If you are still uncertain, the smell of the flowers will reassure. The aroma is that of muscat – glorious, sweet, rich and heady. Indeed it is too heady for some. Many detect a certain sickliness; perhaps even a whiff of cat's wee. There is something in these accusations, so if you are a sensitive soul, pick the blossoms before the heat of the day has brought on their full potency. If you can *only* smell cat's wee you probably have a Rowan tree on your hands. Only pick the fully open flowers, which retain the rich yellow stamens in the centre. Over-the-hill blossoms are always a little grey and drop their petals easily.

The flower heads can be cut with scissors or simply snapped off at the first joint. Once you have enough, go home straight away and start work – fresh Elder blossoms do not keep well. I usually remove the fresh flowers from their green umbels with a fork – not worrying too much about the occasional green bit of stalk. If I am making a Champagne I will chuck the whole flower head into the pot. The berries too can be removed with a fork.

If you are unable to deal with your collection immediately, it is possible to dry it. Indeed it is wise to dry as many flowers as you can as they retain their aroma quite well and provide a supply into the next season. Place the umbels upside down on a flat surface and leave in a warm dry place out of the sunlight. The dried flowers come away easily from the stems – just shake. Since Elderflowers are always used as an infusion, dried petals can be employed in just the same way as fresh ones.

There is no hedgerow glory finer than the Elderflower. As a Champagne, cordial or sorbet it is a treat beyond compare. Yet I think it is still under-used – supermarket shelves are not overburdened with Elderflower yogurt or Elderflower ice lollies. At home, of course, the limits are set only by our imaginations, a particularly successful exercise of which resulted in my proudest creation – Elderflower Delight (p.232). A few more suggestions are: a jelly (with added lemon juice, or even Sorrel, to lend some bite), a syrup to go on pancakes or ice cream (p.237), a mousse or even some blossoms tied in a cloth and added to your bath (a bit girly this one, forget I said it). The best Elderflower recipes bring in another hedgerow treasure – the Gooseberry. Gooseberry jam infused in the final boiling stage with a muslin bag of Elderflowers is just wonderful, and Gooseberry and Elderflower fool is a dessert made in heaven.

Apart from their familiar use in Elderberry wine, the berries are a little more of a challenge. They are mildly poisonous raw so they should always be cooked. There was a tradition that Elderberries were as good as grapes until their unfortunate encounter with Judas Iscariot; now they are rather tart and pippy. Despite this they have a good fruity flavour and will make a passable jelly, especially when mixed with Blackberries. Elderberries always seem halfway to vinegar when you pick them and this quality can be exploited in a superb Elderberry vinegar. My favourite way of using them, however, is simply as a juice. Cook a kilo of berries, strain through a sieve and add sugar (quite a bit) to taste. It is one of the best hedgerow drinks and puts all that imported cranberry juice to shame.

Dandelion *Taraxacum* agg.

DESCRIPTION	Small perennial. Rosette up to 30cm across. Leaves sharply indented with saw-toothed edges, hairless. Flowers rise on hollow stems from the centre. Flowers bright orange-yellow, composite. Stems and leaves produce a bitter white latex
HABITAT	Recently disturbed grassland, wasteland, roadsides
DISTRIBUTION	Extremely common everywhere
SEASON	Leaves best in spring before the main flower crop, which is between late March and early May. The occasional flower can be found through much of the year. Roots in autumn and winter

I think that most people have a deep affection for the Dandelion; along with the daisy, it is a wild flower that even the most urban of urbanites will recognise. There has certainly been a great deal of appreciative, but truly terrible poetry written in its honour:

> *Said young Dandelion,*
> *With a sweet air,*
> *I have my eye on*
> *Miss Daisy fair.*

and purple prose:

> *When the children of the plant arrive at maturity, each one of them with*
> *parental care is furnished with a handsome balloon filled with provisions;*
> *a gust of wind separates the family…*

A field of Dandelions is indeed a wonderful sight, so we must forgive such excess. For the forager the Dandelion is a treasure. It provides three crops – leaves, roots and flowers. The leaves can be collected at any time, but they are less bitter and more crunchy just before the flowers appear. The roots are best disinterred in the autumn or winter when they will be at their plumpest. It is possible to find the odd Dandelion flower at all but the coldest times of the year, but the main flush happens in early spring. Gather them in the morning, in full sun if possible, then rush home and deal with them straight away before they close up for the night. There are numerous similar-looking plants, such as the catsears and hawkbits, but the flowers of these tend to be smaller and are not toxic should you make a mistake.

The Dandelion has long been collected for its medicinal benefits. It is, above all things, a diuretic; a talent confirmed by modern science and probably down to its high potassium content. Its unfortunate common name of 'piss-a-bed' testifies to this reputation. The huge number of ailments it is reputed to cure is largely a matter of wishful thinking, but it *is* an exceptionally healthy food, containing vitamins A, C and K, along with potassium and calcium and a reasonable amount of protein.

The leaves should be collected before the flowers appear, but they are always rather bitter. Mixed with milder salad plants, however, they provide an acceptable bite to a sandwich. The intensity of the bitterness can be reduced by covering the young leaves with a pot for a few days to force them – though this is perilously close to gardening and not entirely in the spirit of the book.

The flowers have a limited use in the kitchen – they make an interesting (i.e. horrible) tea, or they can be dipped in batter and fried to make fritters (even more horrible). One recipe that works very well is Dandelion Jelly Marmalade (p.240) as the petals impart a pleasant bitterness and colour; the petals also make an excellent floral syrup (p.237). Where they really come into their own, however, is in Dandelion wine – one of the best of all the country wines.

The roots are very bitter raw and just about edible cooked. They are best known for their use in Dandelion and burdock beer. One other odd use is well known though seldom tried – Dandelion coffee. The roots are scrubbed, dried thoroughly in a low oven, then roasted at 200°C/Gas mark 6 for 30 minutes and then ground up like coffee. This is the sort of report that no sensible person will ever believe but for once it is true – it genuinely works. The result is almost indistinguishable from real coffee in smell, appearance and taste, lacking perhaps just some of the more subtle aromas. It contains no caffeine of course so you will be able to get to sleep very easily. How long for, though, is another matter – just remember that vulgar common name.

P.S. The agg. part of the Dandelion's Latin name given above is an abbreviation of 'aggregate'. This means that we are talking about several microspecies – in this case (the British Isles) no less than 235 – from *T. aberrans* to *T. xiphoideum*. You may well have noticed that not all Dandelions are the same – some larger, some smaller, some with sharply serrated leaves, some more rounded and so on. Among the general mass of botanists there is a small band who live on a higher plane than their colleagues and study nothing but Dandelions. They are called Taraxacologists. Two of these grand masters, Dudman and Richards, in their great work *Dandelions of Great Britain and Ireland*, say that they suspect other botanists consider them mad. How right they are. But to study a subject of interest to no one but a tiny coterie and which is, as far as we can tell, totally inconsequential, is strangely commendable. *Salute*, taraxacologists!

Several other common plants are apomictic (as this microspeciation is called), most famously the Blackberry, which has a subspecies for every day of the year. Apomictic species have all but given up sex as a messy waste of time and effort and their offspring are nearly always clones. This is a slightly dangerous strategy for, although the overheads involved in sexual reproduction no longer have to be borne, the advantages of genetic interchange and the removal of harmful mutations are lost. However, they dabble in sex occasionally, which prevents them entering an evolutionary dead end. Parthenogenesis (meaning virgin birth) in certain animals, such as stick insects and some lizards, is a related process.

With the Dandelions it seems that a huge number of these microspecies were created thousands of years ago and their genetic makeup became fixed seemingly for ever. The weakest became extinct, leaving us with the few hundred we have now.

Wild Plum *Prunus domestica*

DESCRIPTION	Small tree or shrub. Leaves pointed/oval, coarse blunt-toothed edges, slightly hairy both sides, alternate. Thornless. Fruit with bloom, purple, sometimes green or yellow, groove on one side
HABITAT	Hedgerows, wood edges, often naturalised around deserted buildings
DISTRIBUTION	Fairly common everywhere, except central northern England and the Scottish Highlands
SEASON	September–October

Cherry Plum *P. cerasifera*

DESCRIPTION	Small tree or shrub. Leaves pointed/oval, blunt but *finely* toothed edges, slightly hairy on underside of midrib, alternate. Mostly thornless. Fruit the size and shape of a very large cherry, but with a typical plum groove down one side. Red or yellow
HABITAT	Hedgerows – frequently planted, often near habitation
DISTRIBUTION	Common throughout the British Isles, though much more so in the Midlands and the Southeast
SEASON	July

There are variations within *Prunus domestica* that have attained subspecies status but they are unclear and inconsistent and hybrids between them confuse the picture further. Plums can therefore be confusing, but for all practical purposes (we just want to eat them) Plums, Bullaces and Damsons are the same thing. Cherry Plums, however, are not, and I will talk about them separately.

Wild Plum trees are hot property and if you find one it is best not to mention it to your 'friends'. Pick the Plums as ripe as you can, remembering that someone else may be watching the tree. There will be particularly enticing fruit out of reach at the top, and ladders, fruit-pickers and even standing on the roof of your car may be required. If the tree is safe from other foragers you can place a large sheet on the ground to catch fallen fruit, but not for long – they will not be safe from animals.

Wild Plum

Cherry Plum

The Cherry Plum is a sadly overlooked fruit – passed by as an inedible unknown, fallen and squashed on the roadside. It has very early blossoms – the beginning of March being typical and long before nearly any other tree. Herein lies the problem with Cherry Plums. The blossoms are often affected by cold weather and fail to set. If it is mild at the right time, however, you can look forward to an extraordinarily large crop. In July the fruit will hang like grapes from the tree, the branches brought to breaking point with their colourful burden, and it can be difficult to carry home all you have picked. Time, perhaps, for reinforcements.

Both Plums are enormously variable in texture and taste, as was noted in typically outrageous fashion by Culpeper:

> All plums are under Venus, and are, like women, some better, some worse.

This is due as much to growing conditions and time of picking as species and variety, but it is true that Plums can, indeed, delight or disappoint in equal measure. There is never any way of guessing what a Plum will taste like – you will just have to eat it. I have, however, consistently found the yellow Cherry Plums to possess a superior flavour to the red.

All Plums will suit recipes for their cultivated sisters. Jams and jellies, Plum wine and Plum gin, crumble and cake, pudding and pie, bottled or dried – there is really no need to detail the many ways you can cook with Plums – it is just that the flavour is so much better for being freely acquired.

P.S. Geneticists must have larger brains than the rest of us in order to carry around the endless amount of detail encountered in their discipline. Nothing in genetics is ever easy; every rule has an exception and the only firm rule is that there isn't one. *Prunus domestica* is the name of the cultivated plum and the wild form is the same species escaped from the garden. Most organisms (including us) have two sets of chromosomes but some, including a large number of plants, are not content and will have more. This is called polyploidy and is important. *Prunus domestica* has no less than six and is thus referred to as being hexaploid. These six sets come from three ancestors. It is possible that four of them came from two Blackthorns and two from a Cherry Plum but more likely that all six are former Cherry Plum chromosomes. If the latter is the case then Wild Plums are *super* Cherry Plums.

Chromosomes contain most of an organism's DNA and control most of what goes on inside the cell. One would think that having more than your fair share of chromosomes would be like having three cooks in the kitchen – miserable confusion. But it is generally not so and polyploid organisms are often, like our plum, large and vigorous. We have much to thank this quirk of nature for: potatoes, wheat, oats, sugar cane, bananas, and many more food species have been developed using artificially induced polyploidy.

Yarrow *Achillea millefolium*

DESCRIPTION	Medium/short, upright perennial, to 50cm when flowering. Leaves very feather-like. Flowers in an umbrella of florets, which have five white petals and a yellow centre
HABITAT	Grassy banks, garden borders, hedges and grassland
DISTRIBUTION	Very common throughout the British Isles
SEASON	May–November

The strikingly feather-like leaves can be found growing in amongst grass almost everywhere and you are very likely to have some in your garden.

The Latin name derives from the Greek hero Achilles, who was supposed to have learned from his centaur mentor Chiron about its beneficial properties as a herb for healing battle wounds. Not a particularly effective one, evidently, considering Achilles' fate. The second part of the Latin name is a plain description of the leaves - 'thousand-leaved'.

Yarrow normally finds only one use in the kitchen. I have been particularly scathing of herbal teas and generally speaking I think they deserve it. Yarrow tea, however, is really quite good, I will put it no stronger than that, and I feel it is one can recommend.

Crow Garlic *Allium vineale*

DESCRIPTION	Medium perennial, 30–60cm. Leaves stiff, grass-like, semi-cylindrical, hollow and grooved. Flowers mixed with the bulbils (tiny bulbs) or just bulbils, these emerging from a papery sheath. Underground bulb, onion-like, 1–2cm diameter
HABITAT	Grassy banks, field edges, cultivated land
DISTRIBUTION	Common in southern England, except the moors in the Southwest. Rare in Northern Ireland. Largely coastal elsewhere and increasingly scarce in the North
SEASON	Leaves during winter and spring, bulbs late spring and early summer

Some plants are revered, some reviled. Crow Garlic is definitely in the latter camp. The word garlic comes, it is believed, from the Anglo-Saxon *gār lēac* meaning 'spear leek' – a reference to the leaf shape of cultivated garlic. Crow Garlic comes from *crāwan lēac* meaning 'crows' leek' – a leek fit only for crows.

In fact it was not the flavour of Crow Garlic that gave it such a poor reputation, it is what it did to milk. Crow Garlic has always been a common weed of pasture and cows will eat it with the grass. Even a small amount makes the milk from these animals undrinkable, so a great deal of effort was expended in eradicating it from the land. It was not only milk that was spoiled. Wheat could also become contaminated; it seems that garlic bread was sometimes on the menu long before it became fashionable or desirable. A gossip paper from 1796 has some '*Ironical Advice to Bakers*', suggesting that as well as ground bones the baker should also use '*cheap wheats that are plentifully mixed with crow-garlick*' because of its '*excellent perfume*' and '*leeky flavour*' which will be much requested by his Welsh customers. In 1736 there was even a complaint that the truffles found in Richmond Park were tainted with the odour of nearby Crow Garlic. In fact truffles naturally have a slight garlicky flavour due to some related organic sulphur compounds.

None of this need worry the forager, who will be welcome in places where it is unwanted. In southern England it is common in hedgerows and grassy places, especially near the sea. One problem with foraging for this plant is seeing it, even if it is in front of you. The leaves are just like those of a coarse grass – a near perfect, accidental camouflage. As with most foraged items you will soon learn their subtle differences of growth habit and shape. Early spring is a good time to collect Crow Garlic as the leaves stand in clearly visible clumps above the still sleeping grass.

The leaves have a good, chive-like flavour but they are a bit stringy unless very young. The best crop from Crow Garlic, however, is the bulb. This can be difficult to dig up from amongst the dense grass in which it often grows, but if the flower stem is visible you can use it as a handle to uproot the whole plant. The bulb looks like a silverskin onion but tastes halfway between garlic and onion. It can be used – raw or cooked – with discretion, in place of either. The flavour is not as strong as garlic so you can use more in your recipe.

Wild Garlic *Allium ursinum*

DESCRIPTION	Short/medium perennial, to 50cm. Leaves broadly elliptical and pointed, soft and often damp to the touch. Flowers white, star-like, five-petalled in round sprays. All parts smell strongly of garlic
HABITAT	Shaded hedgerow, woodland
DISTRIBUTION	Very common throughout the British Isles, except for the north of Scotland. Also less common in central eastern England
SEASON	Leaves February–June. Flowers and seed heads April– June. Root bulb all year, if you can find them

Wild Garlic, or Ramsons as it is also known, is a wild food that nearly everyone has heard of, even if they have never seen it. This is an extremely common plant and a gift of nature to the wild gourmet. From March until June shady roadsides and open woodlands are filled with the elegant lanceolate leaves and in May and June the pretty star-shaped flowers. They are also filled with the smell of garlic. This is pleasant enough in small amounts and at the beginning of the season, but as the leaves start to disintegrate, it becomes rancid and overpowering. While the culinary possibilities of this plant were not unknown it was more often used in the past for its medical virtues:

> *Eate leekes in Lide, and ramsins in May,*
> *And all the yeare after physitians may play.*

In this old West Country rhyme 'Lide' is a name for March. The health-giving properties of garlic in its several forms are well known – antioxidant, antiseptic and more – but its true potential in the kitchen has only relatively recently been appreciated in this country.

Wild Garlic abounds in the countryside but it is not particularly happy in an urban environment, preferring shaded hedgerows and open woods. The younger the leaves the better they will be – certainly try to pick them before they flower – after this the flavour becomes fainter and coarser. When you find your patch you will have an over-abundance of riches, as there will be many more than you can possibly eat. Scissors are a must for picking the leaves and a largish flat basket will help keep them safe. If you have travelled to your picking spot by car you may encounter a small problem – unless the smell of garlic is to you a joy beyond compare do not put your collection on the back seat – a warm car can bring out the overwhelming best

(or worst) that Wild Garlic has to offer. The leaves wilt very quickly so either use them as soon as you get home or keep them covered in the fridge.

It is the leaves which are almost invariably eaten, but the decorative flowers and the young seed heads are also edible, both tasting strongly of garlic. Whether or not the leaves are around, it is still possible to gather the underground bulb – even in December. This tubular structure is a modified leaf stem and similar in flavour to a familiar garlic bulb, if a little milder. Do take all the necessary legal and safety precautions for collecting wild roots.

There are, unfortunately, several poisonous plants which lie in wait for the careless Wild Garlic collector. Lily of the valley bears a striking similarity to Wild Garlic and is a common garden plant occasionally found escaped to the wild. Do be careful, therefore, if picking near habitation as it is quite seriously poisonous. The Autumn Crocus (or Meadow Saffron) also has long pointed leaves and has caused at least one death in the UK quite recently after being mistaken for Wild Garlic. Much more common is Lords and Ladies (p.191). The fully grown leaves are quite unlike those of Wild Garlic but the immature ones could confuse, especially as they too appear from the barren ground of early spring. This may all sound rather worrying but there is no need for concern – Wild Garlic smells strongly of garlic when crushed and none of these impostors do.

Wild Garlic is considerably milder in flavour than its cultivated cousin, but it can be used in all the familiar situations. As it is used mostly in the form of a leaf however, it does provide some extra culinary avenues to explore. Two simple uses come straight away to mind – chopped in a salad or whole in a cheese sandwich. Finely chopped it looks great mixed into cream cheese or in an omelette. Perhaps one of the best recipes is Wild Garlic Pesto (p.205) – a real wild delight. A wild British version of the Greek dolma, Wild Garlic Parcels (p.204), can be made from the larger leaves.

P.S. It is a strange but fortuitous fact that the tasty members of the lily family (onions, garlic, chives, Wild Garlic and many others) are edible to humans. We are almost unique in the animal kingdom in finding them both palatable and non-toxic. Most animals will not happily touch them (sheep are apparently an exception) and when forced through circumstance to eat them may be poisoned. Most dog and cat owners know not to give their animals onions in any form – a compound *n-propyl disulphide* causes serious anaemia and deaths have occurred.

Grazing animals will commonly eat a little Wild Garlic and, more commonly still, small amounts of Crow Garlic. This seldom causes ill health in the animal, but its milk will be undrinkable and, if some is consumed just prior to slaughter, the meat will be spoiled.

Hazel *Corylus avellana*

DESCRIPTION	Small tree or shrub. Sometimes single stem, more often multiple stems. Leaves large and roundish, but with a pointed end. Stems straight, grey-brown, horizontal markings. The flowers in catkins. Nuts enclosed in overlapping bracts, in clusters of two, three or four
HABITAT	Understorey in broad-leaved woods, hedgerow, scrub
DISTRIBUTION	Very common throughout the British Isles, save the odd mountain top
SEASON	Nuts late August until mid-October

We all have our favourite places. Mine is a Hazel coppice about a mile from where I live in Dorset. It is a peaceful place with overarching ash trees, snuffling, scratching badger cubs in April, a dazzling carpet of bluebells in May and some rare, if inedible, fungi in October. The wood was established centuries ago to supply fencing and hurdles for the local sheep farms, but hurdles are mostly, though not entirely, a thing of the past. Nowadays the Hazels, some more than 2 metres across, wait in vain for the coppicer's lopper. In the dark centre of the coppice few nuts ripen, but the trees at its bright edge sometimes produce more than I can pick.

The wild Hazelnut is the ancestor of the large, carefully cultivated cobnut, which appears in the shops in August and September. There are around seventy varieties but they are still all *Corylus avellana*. This gentle form of agriculture once thrived in Kent, but is now much reduced from its heyday, so do supplement your wild harvest by buying them when you see them in the shops. There are also filberts (named after St Philibert whose feast day, 20 August, coincides with the start of the nutting season). These large nuts are a different species (*C. maxima*), which seldom grows wild in the British Isles.

Wild native Hazelnuts have been picked since antiquity, but few people bother with them now and it can indeed be a frustrating exercise. The hedgerow-grown Hazel sometimes produces nuts but most will have been lost to the voracious council hedge-trimmer. Of course hedges have two sides and you may be luckier if you venture on to the field side if there is one. Untrimmed woodland edges like my own patch are the best hunting grounds. It will probably not be news to you that squirrels eat nuts and they do take a fair toll of the crop; but if there are enough nuts about, the squirrels simply cannot get round to eating them all – even squirrelling them away. You could solve the problem by eating the squirrels (only grey ones!) – they are rather good and squirrel offal kebabs are among the best things I have tasted. If

you manage to find a tree covered in nuts you may still face disappointment. Many of the nuts are empty, or 'blank' or 'hedge' nuts as the Kentish growers call them, though unfortunately it is not possible to tell this until you crack them open. Some years are excellent, however, producing a bumper crop with most of the shells full.

The nuts are edible as soon as they reach a good size in August and early September. The early green nuts are milky and slightly fruity in taste but lack the oily richness of the mature nut. They do not keep or ripen further once picked, so eat them straight away. One advantage with the green nuts is that the squirrels seldom bother with them. The fully ripe nut is brown and tends to fall off the branch as soon as you look at it with any degree of anticipation. I often bring a blanket with me to catch these strays. You can also shake the tree to dislodge the ripest nuts but it is hard work for a poor result. It will be well worth checking a few nuts as you go to make sure you do not go home with a basket full of empty shells.

Ripe Hazelnuts will keep for several months, but my wild crop is very precious and gets eaten as soon as I can find the time (or someone else) to shell them. However, this does mean that you are released from the yoke of seasonality and can use them long after their growing season. As with most wild food you will want to do something special with them.

Several recipes in this book use Hazelnuts to their very best effect – ground to make the pastry case for Cranberry and Apple Tart (p.222) and sprinkled artistically on to Chestnut Macaroons (p.231). You can also use them instead of Pignuts in Wild Garlic Pesto (p.205). One odd use which works best with the fresh nuts is Hazelnut milk. The basic method is to soak a handful in water overnight, rinse, then blitz them in a blender with about 400ml water or skimmed milk. Strain through a muslin bag and drink.

Sweet Chestnut *Castanea sativa*

DESCRIPTION	Large tree. Leaves large, long, pointed/oval, saw-toothed edge. Husk covered with very sharp spines. Nuts two or more to a husk, slightly hairy!
HABITAT	Park or woodland. Not on lime
DISTRIBUTION	Common, scattered around England but with a southern preference. Less common in Scotland, Northern Ireland and central Wales
SEASON	October

Like so many plants that are not native to the British Isles the Sweet Chestnut is less than perfectly at home here, even after two thousand years. The nut is often unformed and even when it does reach an edible size is rarely more than a third of the size of its southern European sister, the single nutted marron. Also, it seldom grows from self-set seed in this cooler clime, normally having to be planted. Not that the tree itself appears to struggle – Sweet Chestnuts are among our most impressive trees, some many centuries old and vast in size.

Sweet Chestnuts of an edible size are not necessarily found every year, but sometimes the weather suits them and we get a bumper crop. The ones pictured here are genuine Dorset Chestnuts, a very good size – and very sweet. A search around the forest floor in September and early October will often find hundreds of husks containing pathetically small or unformed Chestnuts. These are usually just nuts that the tree has discarded, saving its energies for the remaining fruits, which will contain useable nuts. These should be ripe and ready in the second half of October. Sometimes only one or two trees in a forest will set good fruit, so do not be too despondent if the first few trees you find produce only empty husks.

There is nothing to confuse the would-be Chestnut gatherer beyond the obvious and unrelated Horse Chestnut or conker tree. I think it a pity that the substantial nut of the latter is not edible and have tried to find out if there is a way of removing the toxin; there isn't. If you're in any doubt, the husk of the Sweet Chestnut is covered in a large number of long, fine bristles and contains more than one nut, whereas the Horse Chestnut has a few rather stumpy spines and only ever contains a single nut. Sweet Chestnut spines are extremely sharp, '*As troublesome to handle as a hedgehog*', as an eighteenth-century writer has it, and the husk cannot be held even gently without a finger being pricked. Rubber or leather gloves are the best defence against this peril. The traditional method of removing the nuts is to make a small pile in the woods, stamp on it and search through the debris for the bright shiny treasure.

The Chestnut is a sadly neglected food, seldom used in Britain other than around Christmas. The seventeenth-century writer and gardener Evelyn laments: '*But we give that fruit to our swine in England, which is amongst the delicacies of princes in other countries.*' I have tried to compensate for this continuing oversight by providing no less than four recipes that use Chestnuts (see below).

Finding carbohydrates is always a problem for the forager – fruits and leaves contain little, and roots are often more trouble than they are worth. Chestnuts, however, contain large amounts – and provide it in a delicious and accessible form. A typical value is around 40 per cent of the fresh peeled weight. The chestnut contains much less fat (3 per cent) than the other wild nut in this book, the Hazelnut (60 per cent); it is fairly light on protein but unusual in containing vitamin C and also some of the B vitamins. Altogether a healthy and useful food. I have a theory that one could survive on my favourite chestnut recipe alone – Chestnuts and Brussels sprouts. 'Alone' is appropriate here.

The Chestnut's sweet, starchy nature allows it to be used with great success in both sweet and savoury dishes. Whether used whole or puréed, chestnuts must be at least part-cooked to make removal of the skin possible. Boil them for 10 minutes in small batches then, using rubber gloves, remove one at a time from the hot water, cut open and peel. Both outer and inner skin will come away easily.

The traditional way of eating Chestnuts of course is by roasting them in the fire. The nuts must have a slit cut in them to release the steam which would otherwise build up to explosive pressures. Richard Mabey's playful suggestion that one Chestnut should be left unslit to indicate when the others are ready should be ignored unless you want lots of holes burnt in your carpet. There is something very special about sitting there, perspiring vigorously, carefully arranging your batches of chestnuts so that they cook just right, then burning your fingers when you try to peel them.

The high starch content is obvious from the crumbly consistency of the cooked nut. This starch enables Sweet Chestnut to be turned into a wonderful flour, making it one of the most versatile wild foods. If you find yourself in possession of a large quantity of the nuts – and time – it is well worth making. Peel slightly undercooked Chestnuts, then flake using a Mouli grater. Dry the flakes in a low oven at 40°C and then pulverise in a blender. This flour can be used for gnocchi, pancakes, biscuits, pasta, polenta, pastry, cakes and even bread, though as it is lacking in gluten it does not rise well and should be used half and half with a strong bread flour. An extremely rich roux can be made using Chestnut flour, and one of the best meals to serve on a cold December evening is a game pie packed with as many woodland creatures as you can get your hands on, the juices thickened with a Chestnut roux.

Finally there is the most famous of all Chestnut treats – marron glacé. See also the recipes for Horseradish and Chestnut Dumplings (p.216), Chestnut Pancakes (p.226), Chestnut Macaroons (p.231) and Chestnut Florentines (p.229).

Juniper *Juniperus communis*

DESCRIPTION	Small tree. Sometimes upright, but more usually sprawling, evergreen. Berries 6mm–1cm diameter, green for a long time, blue/black when ripe. Usually grows in colonies
HABITAT	Dry limestone in the South, acid areas in the North
DISTRIBUTION	Main population in northern Scotland. Also in the north of England, north of Northern Ireland and northern Wales, and in central southern England
SEASON	August–November

The Juniper is one of only three conifers native to the British Isles (Yew and Scots Pine being the others), but despite this it is not really common. It also has an odd distribution pattern. I have never seen one in Dorset outside a garden centre, but in nearby Wiltshire at Britain's very own Area 51 – Porton Down – there are thousands of them, constituting 20 per cent of the southern England population. These are not exactly accessible to the forager. All the trees here are either around one hundred years old or fifty years old, coinciding with periods when rabbit numbers were very low, so it may be that it is rabbits eating the seedling plants that restricts Juniper populations. In Scotland, at least in the northern half, they are much more common and where I found those pictured overleaf.

To be precise the berries are not berries, they are cones; if you look carefully you will see the overlapping layers on the surface. The relatively soft and rather sticky outer layer is sweet and aromatic, while the central part is highly aromatic and crunchy. Eating a plain berry is a little like drinking a straight gin downwind of a pine forest. The gin connection is obvious, of course, because Juniper gives this drink its flavour and indeed its name – from the French for Juniper – *genévrier*. The reputation of gin is a long-standing one, summed up rather well in the *Compleat Confectioner* of 1742:

> *It is indeed true, that the Liquor call'd Geneva, or, more vulgarly, Gin,*
> *becoming of late Years but too common, has been the Occasion of much Mischief*
> *and many Disorders; but the best Things may be abus'd.*

It is probably just as well that the domestic manufacture of gin is illegal and that we must turn our minds to more temperate uses for this unusual food.

Those Juniper trees that can be found are often in ecologically sensitive areas and the tree itself is the subject of various biodiversity action plans. A certain amount of

care and restraint should therefore be exercised when collecting (though how much good this will do if there are rabbits around I cannot say). You will certainly need to take care, as the needles are the sharpest of any plant I know. An alternative to picking by hand is to lay a sheet underneath the tree and shake or beat it, but it is better just to use gloves.

Since Juniper berries are not true berries they cannot be expected to follow a typical berry lifestyle, and indeed they do not. The green berries will remain on the plant for a year or two, only ripening blue/black in the second or third year. Also, different-aged berries can be found on the same branch with maybe just a few ripe ones among the green. As a fairly substantial proportion of trees (mostly the males) do not produce berries, it can sometimes seem a miracle to find a bush that actually has some. Fortunately a few berries go a long way and, providing you can locate some trees in the first place, you should not face an entirely unrewarding quest.

The strong clean flavour of the berry is used to moderate rich, gamey or fatty meats, such as pork, venison and duck. Juniper Pot (p.213), a delicious Danish recipe, uses loin of pork. Marinades, sauces and pickles can all usefully employ the berries and if you want your Sloe Gin (p.82) to taste more of gin than of Sloes then add Juniper berries. Considering the rather medicinal taste, it is unsurprising that Juniper berries have long found a place in the medicine cabinet. They have been employed against the biting of snakes, against dropsy, colic and a dozen or so other ailments. One of the more likely remedies, which I found in an eighteenth-century travelogue, is for a chesty cough. It is this which inspired what is perhaps the most unusual recipe in this book – Juniper Toffee (p.234). Not that I make any claims for its efficacy – it just tastes great.

One small word of warning – Juniper really does contain pharmacologically active compounds, the principal of which is an abortifacient. It has long been employed domestically for this doubtful purpose – copious quantities of gin and a very hot bath being the normal modus operandi. As well as expectant mothers, those suffering kidney problems should also avoid Juniper berries.

Sea Buckthorn *Hippophae rhamnoides*

DESCRIPTION	Shrub or small tree, to 2.5 metres. Leaves long and thin, grey/green with grey dots. Stems thorny. Bright-orange berries in very dense clusters, extremely sharp-tasting
HABITAT	Seashore, sand dunes. Frequently planted elsewhere as a roadside shrub
DISTRIBUTION	Fairly common around the entire coast of Britain, though only native on the east coast. Occasionally inland, mostly through being planted
SEASON	Berries ripe from late July and persist into the winter. Early berries, before the frosts, are by far the best

This striking plant with its intensely bright-orange berries and pretty grey/green leaves is becoming more familiar now that it is being planted as a roadside shrub. It is actually a seaside plant native to the east coast, and if it is seen elsewhere on the coast it has, again, been planted. Sea Buckthorn is useful for firming up sand dunes and providing coastal protection, but a little too good at its job, sometimes turning the ecologically sensitive dunes into dense, impenetrable thickets.

While it may be thoroughly despised by the naturalist, for the forager it is a great delicacy. If it has a drawback it is the near impossibility of picking the berries. The branches are covered in ferocious spines and the berries burst as soon as you touch them. As it is only the juice that is wanted, I usually just squidge it straight into a little plastic tub held underneath the branch and sieve out all the unwanted debris later. Another possibility, which can only be justified where the plants are clearly unwelcome for environmental reasons, is to cut off whole branches with secateurs or even a saw, put them in the freezer and then shake off the frozen berries.

The flavour of Sea Buckthorn berries has to be experienced to be believed. If you have ever eaten what is sometimes called 'extreme candy' you will have a vague idea, though you will have to imagine it without the sugar. The berries contain large quantities of malic acid, a natural acid an order of magnitude sharper than the more familiar citric acid. The juice can be used, diluted and with sugar, to make a spine-stiffening drink, or as a fierce wild substitute for lemon with fish. I make Sea Buckthorn and Crab Apple jam, and, though I say so myself, it is a marvellous work among all nations.

Silver Birch *Betula pendula*

DESCRIPTION	Medium-sized tree. Leaves triangular, base straight with rounded corners, other two sides doubly serrated. Branches drooping. Bark silver/white with dark raised horizontal markings, diamond-shaped on mature trees
HABITAT	Prefers light sandy soil
DISTRIBUTION	Very common, except in the far north of Scotland
SEASON	March and early April

Although most of what a forager looks for can, generally speaking, be gathered legally and with a clear conscience, tapping birch trees may involve a small excursion to the dark side.

Unless the trees are your own or you have permission from the owner, tapping a birch tree always feels like a commando raid and on those (rare) occasions when I put righteousness to one side I will take a daughter with me to act as lookout. The enterprise is made all the more exciting by the necessity of returning to the crime scene the next day to collect the prize. But what is this prize, what can you do with it and is it worth so much damage to your karma?

Birch sap, for it is this that is drawn from the Silver Birch, is easy to collect provided you are well equipped and visit your tree at precisely the right time of year. Birch tapping consists simply of drilling a hole into the side of a tree and guiding the flow of sap into a suitable container. I have tried many ways of doing this but the semi-professional method used by the occasional North American maple tapper is by far the best.

The most critical piece of kit is the spile or spout. You won't find these devices in your local ironmonger's in the UK, so you will have to search online for a supplier. A spile is a tapered tube with a hole at one end and a spout at the other. In the middle there is a hook from which a bucket may be hung. The bucket should ideally be galvanised and with a little hole to attach it to the spile, and a cover to keep the rain out. You will also need a wood bit or auger bit, which should be the diameter of the narrow end of the spile – this ensures a tight fit. A brace, or for the modern forager, a battery-operated drill, a mallet, a container to keep the sap in, and some tapered dry wooden pegs – the pores sealed at the narrow end with candle wax – completes the inventory for the well-equipped birch tapper.

Drilling a hole in a tree and bleeding it for 24 hours requires a healthy specimen with a minimum trunk diameter of 25cm. It should also have had at least a couple of years' rest from the last time it was tapped. The hole should be about a metre from the ground, drilled at a slightly upward angle and about 3cm deep. If the tree is ready the sap will pour out as soon as the drill is halfway in. If no sap appears then stop drilling, drive a prepared plug into the wound and try another tree. If, however, all is well, hammer home your spile, attach the bucket and retire for 24 hours. When you have collected your sap remember to firmly fill the hole with your wooden plug as otherwise the sap will continue to run for several days and the tree may not survive this added imposition.

A single tree may produce up to 5 litres in a day, though half as much is more likely. I usually tap about half-a-dozen trees at the same time as birch sap sours quicker than milk and you cannot stockpile it. You will have to gather all you want while you can as the season is very short. Precisely when a birch tree starts to produce sap will depend a great deal on the weather, but around the second week of March is fairly typical. Overall the season is about a month long and ends a little before the buds start to show green. By this time the character of the sap has changed, and not

for the better – it can have an overpowering popcorn flavour; soon after this it stops altogether. For the best flavour, gather sap as early in the season as you can.

Silver Birch is very easy to identify so you should encounter no problems, even though the leaves will not be on the tree to help you. A closely related species, Downy Birch, (*B. pubescens*), is also widespread if not quite so common. It produces a rather bitter sap but is easily distinguished by its red-brown bark. Several other trees produce a sap, though I have had little success in finding the right time to tap them. Sycamore and Field Maple are both maples and thus related to the North American Sugar Maple. They can produce a more sugary sap than Silver Birch but I have never been able to get any out of them. Walnut can also provide sap but as it is a tree which struggles in the UK anyway it is best to leave it in peace.

If Silver Birch trees were able to express an opinion they would no doubt object to having some of their lifeblood drained away, but it seems to have little effect on their viability as long as it is performed only occasionally and with care.

So what can you do with the stuff now you have 20 litres sat in your kitchen? If you have taken a swig of sap while in the woods you may well be wondering what it is good for – its taste is almost indistinguishable from water. But it is very good water indeed. In Scandinavia, where birch trees grow in astronomical numbers, the sap is bottled and sold as a tonic. It does have a slight flavour, with a hint of sweetness, but both are very faint.

Apart from drinking it straight, there are two other uses for the sap – Birch sap wine and Birch Sap Syrup. A lot of people swear by the wine, but apart from a mild woodiness I suspect it contributes little more than water. No doubt I am betraying an insensitive palate here so I suggest you try it for yourself. Much more interesting is the syrup. This is similar to maple syrup but with its own distinctive flavour – molasses maybe, or caramel with slightly acidic or bitter undertones. It is terrific on pancakes, especially Chestnut Pancakes (p.226), but really comes into its own when used for that 1970s dinner party standby – crème caramel.

The low sugar content of Birch sap (less than 1 per cent) means that an awful lot of water needs to be evaporated off: 10 litres will produce a frankly pitiful 100ml of Birch Sap Syrup if fully concentrated. Sugar Maple by comparison produces two and a half times as much. I start the process in a preserving pan then, when 90 per cent of the water has gone, transfer the thin syrup to a bain-marie, or a heatproof bowl over a saucepan of simmering water. The point of this is to prevent the fructose-rich syrup burning. (Make sure the bowl is a big one – you will need to get your head inside to lick it out later.) If you continue reducing you will obtain a sticky brown substance. This is strong-flavoured and bitter, so, if you are unconcerned about authenticity, it is better to stop the process earlier and add some white sugar – the Birch sap effectively being used as a flavouring. As long as it is sticky enough it will keep well in a sealed bottle – certainly the full ten months until next Pancake Day.

Bulrush/Reedmace *Typha latifolia*

DESCRIPTION	Tall upright perennial grass, 1–2.5m. Leaves in two rows, topmost extend above the flower head. Stem enclosed in the leaves, up to 4cm in diameter, completely round in cross-section. Male flower spike directly above the thicker female flower spike
HABITAT	Swampy areas, ditches, garden ponds
DISTRIBUTION	Frequent in England, except the Northwest. Occasional in Scottish and Welsh lowlands and Northern Ireland
SEASON	Early spring for the young shoots

I become unaccountably excited whenever I see a stand of Bulrushes. All other large grasses seem like poor impostors, but for some reason the Bulrush seems like the real thing. Beyond its beauty there is another reason to love this plant – you can eat it. Although by no means as common as it once was – due to the drainage of wetland for agriculture – Bulrushes are still a familiar sight in the countryside, especially the English countryside.

It is, however, not a plant I would recommend collecting whenever you find it – its habitat is often a delicate one and may even be protected. Also, since you will have to remove nearly all of the plant you may need permission from the landowner in order to comply with the law on uprooting plants. Nevertheless, it can sometimes be found in large quantities and the collecting of half a dozen for the kitchen once or twice a year is unlikely to do any harm. Because they look so attractive Bulrushes have frequently been planted in domestic ponds – a habitat they love not wisely but too well, and the hapless pond-owner may be delighted to see you take away as many of the damn things as you wish.

For some reason almost no one collects this plant for food, yet much of it is edible. The strange rope-like roots contain a great deal of starch, which can be eaten raw or baked to make a flour; the immature flower spike can be eaten raw or cooked and tastes like sweetcorn; one can make flour out of the mature seeds; even the pollen can be collected. In my opinion, however, the best way to eat Bulrushes is to cook the young spring shoots.

A Bulrush patch will be easy to spot, even in early spring, as last year's highly distinctive maces will still be around. From late February to April or even May the young shoots will grow from the starch-rich underground roots. Shoots 50–80cm tall are about the right size. They can be cut off at any distance from the roots, but

Distinctive cross-section pattern of the Bulrush shoot

I get my knife right into the mud and cut at the bottom of the stem. The shoots look almost exactly like leeks and are prepared for cooking in the same way.

With last year's seed heads as a clue, it is difficult to confuse Bulrushes with anything else. However, the young yellow flag iris is superficially similar and can cause severe gastrointestinal upsets if eaten. The plant resembles the young Bulrush but the stem is flattened in cross-section instead of perfectly round.

If you have ever sat, bored to distraction, at the edge of a cricket pitch watching a dull game, you may have tried to alleviate the tedium by nibbling on the succulent base of a piece of grass. The flavour is exactly what you get from Bulrush shoots, but of course the size is much greater. A decent-sized shoot will be 3–4cm across, and not much less when the tough outer layers have been peeled back. If you would rather reduce the grassy flavour to a more moderate level, the peeled shoots can be chopped and stir-fried – not unlike bamboo shoots. One of the best stir-fries I ever ate was Bulrush shoots, seaweed, Crow Garlic and Jelly Ear mushrooms (p.203) – an extraordinary combination of wild, and *only* wild, ingredients.

Also look out for several other reeds and rushes. Common Sedge (*Carex nigra*) is the easiest to spot, with its black flowers and three-sided stem. It is much smaller than a Bulrush but there will still be a reasonable amount of succulent stem left after peeling and it is sufficiently common to permit picking a dozen or so.

P.S. Many of you will have noticed that I am following popular usage in calling this plant a Bulrush despite the insistence of many that this name should be restricted to a different grass-like species, *Schoenoplectus lacustris*. What I am calling a Bulrush should, it is said, be called a Great Reedmace. In making my stand I am following Richard Mabey, who calls this a '*rare victory for common English over botanical protocol*'. The Botanical Society of the British Isles hedges its bets by accepting enough names to satisfy and annoy everyone – Bulrush, Great Reedmace and even False Bulrush.

The confusion has long been blamed on the famous late-nineteenth-century painter of 'Victorians in togas', Sir Lawrence Alma-Tadema. The accusation, frequently repeated, is that his painting *Moses in the Bulrushes* depicts the baby Moses nestling in a clump of Great Reedmace and that this image has so imprinted itself on the common mind that the misconception has continued to this day.

The main problem with this nice story is that Alma-Tadema never produced a painting called *Moses in the Bulrushes*. He did, however, paint one called *The Finding of Moses*. Unfortunately this contains neither 'true' Bulrush nor Reedmace. Furthermore, the confusion, if confusion it be, predates not only the painting but also the painter. In 1819, seventeen years before Alma-Tadema's birth, a writer complains of '*reed mace*' being '*vulgarly called bulrush*.'

It is probable that artists when painting the biblical scene have merely continued this 'vulgar' tradition. For example, in 1828 Delaroche paints unmistakable Reedmaces (and a Pharaoh's daughter who seems to be having a little trouble with her clothing) in his depiction of the story.

Still, I am of the opinion that if something has been popularly called by a name for getting on for two hundred years we might as well stick with it.

As it happens neither Reedmace nor the true Bulrush (*S. lacustris*) would have been found in ancient Egypt – a fact apparently known to Alma-Tadema. The infant Moses would have been discovered amongst papyrus (*Cyperus papyrus*). One final, unhelpful twist in this tale is the fact that the word Bulrush comes from the Middle English *bulrish* meaning papyrus.

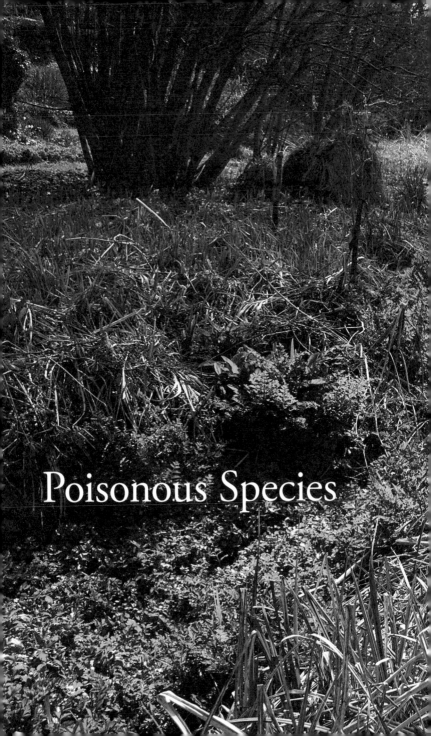

Poisonous Species

Foxglove, *Digitalis purpurea*

Alongside 'don't play with matches', 'remember to clean your teeth' and mind the cat', something that most children learn at their mother's knee is 'never eat wild berries or plants'. Childhood lessons are difficult to unlearn. I was in my twenties when I found out that it wasn't a criminal offence for men to thread a needle – my mother having told me as a five-year-old that it was. But if you want to enjoy what nature has put before us you will have to put aside parental pleas and your own fears. Of course, mothers are right on most things and there is a very real danger in eating wild plants – if you get it wrong, even once, you can die.

A positive identification of an edible plant is essential if you want to eat it, but it is very encouraging if you can also assure yourself that it is not some deadly look-alike. There are more than two hundred poisonous plants in the UK, so I have selected just those that could conceivably present a problem to the forager; they may look like an edible species or they happen to be very common. I have tried to indicate how poisonous each plant is with a star rating. 'X' plants make you quite ill, 'XX' make you very ill and 'XXX' make you dead.

Two families dominate this section – the carrot family and the potato family, more properly called the Umbelliferaceae and the Solanaceae respectively. These are highly ambivalent families – in addition to their many seriously poisonous members, both contain several important edible species as their names carrot and potato suggest. Some of the edible Umbelliferaceae grow wild in Britain, but, apart from the odd self-sown urban tomato, there are no wild edible Solanaceae here – they are all poisonous or unpalatable and usually both. The most serious Solanaceae, Deadly Nightshade, is quite rare and resembles nothing edible. The worst of the Umbelliferaceae is the most deadly of all British plants, very common, *and* looks a bit like several edible species. It is Hemlock Water-dropwort and if you want to collect leaves or roots it is one you really must learn – if you make a mistake with this plant you could be dead within 3 hours.

As with the poisonous fungi, plants do not come with a little label to tell you whether or not you can eat them. You just have to work out what they are from characteristics such as leaf shape, whether or not it is hairy, number of petals and so on. Refer to the specific advice on how to identify plants under individual entries, bearing in mind the most important thing is never to jump to conclusions. And for more information on identifying plants – and a few extra species – go to www.rivercottage.net/foraging.

Hemlock Water-dropwort

Oenanthe crocata XXX

DESCRIPTION	Medium perennial, 50–150cm tall. Leaflets approximately opposite and with a terminal leaflet, deeply lobed. The narrow young leaf stems sheath the stem, sometimes pink tinged. Stems grooved, hollow, young ones especially exude a strong-smelling, sticky fluid which turns slowly yellow. Flowers form in umbels of separate white half-globes. Clusters of swollen white roots
HABITAT	Wet areas, particularly streams, ditches, marshes, damp path edges
DISTRIBUTION	Common and often abundant south of Oxford and on the whole western side of Britain. Generally coastal in northeast England and east Scotland. Largely absent elsewhere
SEASON	Roots exist all year. Young shoots seen from February, flowers in June and July

This is the most poisonous of all British plants and one of the most poisonous in the world, yet it is sufficiently common to fill large tracts of wetland with its bright-green growth in early spring. Its dread power has long been known as is attested by the numerous and often colourful reports of fatal poisonings over the centuries. Occasionally several fatalities will occur when a group partake in a deadly meal. In 1834 four convicts from Woolwich Prison died and ten others survived after supplementing their meagre rations with the roots of this plant; in 1857 two labourers died horribly, again from eating the roots. Much more recently, in 2002, a group of eight young people on holiday in Argyll narrowly escaped death when they made a more than usually toxic vegetable curry. Fortunately, as the poison is diminished with heat and they ate only a little of the sliced root, they suffered only a very uncomfortable couple of days and made a full recovery.

This is such a common plant in many parts of the country that every forager must learn to recognise it. Deadly Nightshade is famously poisonous but quite a rarity, not easily confused with anything edible – not so Hemlock Water-dropwort. Hogweed, Alexanders, Carrot, Parsnip, Ground Elder and several other plants in this book are all excellent edible species, but they belong to the same treacherous

The swollen, deadly roots of Hemlock Water-dropwort

family as Hemlock Water-dropwort – the carrot family (Umbelliferaceae). These ar
notoriously tricky to tell one from the other and include some of the deadlies
species known. The leaves of Hemlock Water-dropwort are fresh-looking and simila
to flat-leaved parsley. The roots, too, look temptingly tasty and substantial, as yo
can see from the picture, and are (I am told) not too unpleasant in flavour. Apar
from acts of straightforward foolhardiness, it is generally the edible root of th
water-parsnip for which Hemlock Water-dropwort is mistaken. A single bite of th
raw root has been known to cause death. The rule, as always, is only to eat somethin
if you are absolutely sure of its name.

The toxin in Hemlock Water-dropwort, oenanthotoxin, assaults the centra
nervous system, causing vomiting, fast heart rate, abdominal cramps and seizures i
all who partake of it. All parts of the plant are toxic, but the fleshy roots have th
highest concentration of poison, higher still in winter and spring.

Finally it is worth mentioning that there are several other Water-dropworts
mercifully none as deadly as Hemlock Water-dropwort. Most are fairly rare thoug
the Corky Water-dropwort (*O. pimpinelloides*) is quite common in grassland in th
southwest of England. There is little point in learning these relative rarities as ther
is nothing edible in this book with which they can be confused.

Hemlock *Conium maculatum* XXX

DESCRIPTION	Upright biennial up to 2 metres. Leaves fern-like, dark green. Mature stems *red spotted*, hollow and cylindrical. Unpleasant mouse-like smell. Flowers white in an umbel. White tap root
HABITAT	Generally damp places, often coastal. Waste ground, ditches, stream sides, roadsides – especially where salted
DISTRIBUTION	Common throughout the British Isles, but largely absent from higher ground and much of Northern Ireland and Scotland, except for the east coast and eastern lowlands
SEASON	First visible in March, flowers in June and July

This stately plant is famously deadly with at least one famous victim to its name – Socrates. His death, however, was no foraging accident but a judicial execution by poisoning. Capital punishment in the ancient world was generally not a cheerful process and Hemlock poisoning may well have been the best of a bad bunch. Francis Bacon states that '*Hemlock is noted for procuring the least painful Death*', although paralysis followed by respiratory failure while the subject is fully conscious is not without its drawbacks.

Hemlock's distinctive red-spotted stem (*maculatum* means 'spotted' – hence 'immaculate' meaning 'unblemished') and imposing size make it an easy plant to recognise and avoid, and its unpleasant mousey smell has not encouraged careless foraging. Nevertheless, a superficial similarity to parsley and a fleshy root not unlike that of Wild Parsnip have led some to make terrible mistakes. All parts of the plant are poisonous, but the seeds particularly so. The principal toxin in Hemlock is coniine, an alkaloid rather similar to nicotine. It affects the central nervous system, causing respiratory failure.

Modern cases of Hemlock poisoning do occur, but even now are not always accidental – in 2006, for example, a biochemist from Devon committed suicide with a lethal cocktail of Hemlock and alcohol. More common is accidental ingestion – often, and tragically, by children. In 1994 a three-year-old Australian boy died when he ate some he had found in his back garden, and in 2002 a thirteen-year-old girl perished in North America. There is no antidote to the several alkaloid poisons contained within Hemlock, survival depending on the original dose, the victim's constitution and energetic nursing care.

Hemlock stems

Hemlock leaves

One rather absurd way of poisoning yourself would be to follow the advice of a seventeenth-century writer on '*How to make… small birds drunk, that you may take them with your hands*' – you mix grain with Hemlock juice. In fact birds are seldom affected by the poison, but their flesh becomes highly toxic, as some who tried it have discovered. Accidental poisoning from eating wild birds inadvertently tainted with Hemlock became a problem in Italy a few years ago with seventeen cases, four of which were fatal, reported between 1972 and 1990.

Inevitably, so powerful a plant found its way into the ancient medicine chest and is still occasionally used in some (highly doubtful) homeopathic preparations. In the mid-eighteenth century, at the instigation of one Dr Storck of Vienna, it became a fashionable remedy for a variety of tumours before the cure was discovered to be worse than the disease. Hemlock's 'cooling' properties (it causes paralysis) are no doubt the reason Culpeper tells us that '… *applied to the privities, it stops its lustful thoughts*'. Best of all is Boyle (of Boyle's Law fame – the one about pressure and volume in a gas being inversely proportional – though I am sure you remember), who suggests rubbing crushed Hemlock on to the chest '*To reduce flaggy Breasts to a good shape and consistence*'. It worked for me.

Fool's Parsley *Aethusa cynapium* xx

DESCRIPTION	Low to medium annual, to 50cm. Leaves fine and deeply incised, fern-like, hairless. Stems ribbed. Flowers white umbrella spray, with conspicuous *long bracts* hanging down below the flower head. All parts smell unpleasant, especially when crushed
HABITAT	Weed of cultivation, waste ground
DISTRIBUTION	Common in England south of Cumbria, scarcer elsewhere
SEASON	Leaves from June to October

The name Fool's Parsley tells you most of what you need to know about this plant. It is another treacherous member of the carrot family, mimicking some of its edible cousins very well. It does look remarkably like cultivated parsley, though not curly-leaved parsley. If you see it in flower all doubts flee as it has highly distinctive long bracts hanging below the flower heads like a beard.

As Fool's Parsley grows happily, indeed chiefly, in the garden, often alongside its cultivated and harmless relative, it is a blessing that the smell and taste are very unpleasant. If you still manage to make a mistake your final warning comes in the form of a burning sensation in the mouth – the plant's Latin name, *Aethusa*, means 'burning one'. The leaves of Fool's Parsley could conceivably be confused with those of Pignut, but Pignut's edible root is rounded while that of Fool's Parsley is like a tiny parsnip.

It is not quite as poisonous as some other members of the carrot family, though it does contain the toxin found in Hemlock – coniine and causes similar symptoms. A nineteenth-century writer refers to the case of two ladies who '*ate a little of it in a sallad instead of parsley, and who were soon seized with nausea, vomiting, headache, giddiness, somnolency, pungent heat in the mouth, throat, and stomach, difficulty in swallowing, and numbness of the limbs*'. It appears that they survived the experience. In 1845 three children ate the roots of Fool's Parsley, thinking them to be parsnips. Two survived, but Ellen Williams, aged just five, died within a few hours. The doctor, one Evan Thomas, House Surgeon to King's College, who reported this incident became fascinated by the plant and its effects and went on to perform some particularly gruesome and fatal experiments on cats and dogs. Modern cases of poisoning are rare and we must hope they stay that way.

Dog's Mercury

Annual Mercury

Dog's Mercury *Mercurialis perennis* xx

DESCRIPTION	Short to medium upright perennial, to 35cm, growing from underground rhizomes. Leaves pointed/oval, opposite, bluntly serrated edge, slightly downy. Flowers on stalks, no petals, whitish
HABITAT	Shady woods and hedges. Forms large patches of vegetation
DISTRIBUTION	Very common throughout the British Isles, save the Fens and northern Scotland
SEASON	From February, but can be found in sheltered locations all year

Annual Mercury *M. annua* x

DESCRIPTION	Short to medium, upright annual, to 50cm. Sometimes branched. Leaves pointed/oval, more coarsely serrated than Dog's Mercury, paler green. Flowers on stalks, white
HABITAT	Weed of cultivation
DISTRIBUTION	Common in England south of the Wash, except Devon and Cornwall. Rare or absent elsewhere
SEASON	May–November. Sometimes overwinters

These closely related species have an uncertain culinary reputation. Dog's Mercury is certainly poisonous, but Annual Mercury was once eaten as a green vegetable and my inclusion of it here in the poisonous section may be a slur on its good character. However, it does have a medical reputation as a 'useful laxative' and this alone may give one pause.

Dog's Mercury is a fairly distinctive plant growing in a distinctive manner in a distinctive habitat so there really should be no reason why anyone would mistake it for anything edible. But, of course, they have. The most reported story of poisoning by this plant is from 1693 when an entire family from Shropshire was laid low with a dinner of Dog's Mercury and bacon; everyone recovered fully save one daughter who sadly perished. There are scattered reports of poisonings over the centuries, including – in 1831 – three women in Boston who mistook the plant for Good King Henry (p.59), a common edible plant of their native Ireland (or '*sweet isle of their nativity*' as the *Boston Medical Journal* prettily puts it). They all survived. Much more recently – in the 1980s – a couple in North Wales mistook Dog's Mercury for Brooklime (p.128). Quite how they managed this I cannot guess, but they suffered severe gastrointestinal problems, inflammation of the kidneys, flushing of the cheeks and jaw, and destruction of some of their red blood cells (haemolysis). Although they consumed a large quantity they were fortunate in that they cooked it first, thus destroying some of the toxins. They made a complete recovery.

Dog's Mercury is very different from Brooklime but it has a resemblance to some of the goosefoots, such as Good King Henry and Many-seeded Goosefoot. Both have tiny flowers on spikes and similar-looking mature leaves arranged around a central stem. The names of these two unrelated groups of plants have intertwined in the past, so that Good King Henry was once known as English Mercury, Annual Mercury as French Mercury and Dog's Mercury (in Germany) as Bad Henry. If that is not enough confusion for you, both Dog's and Annual Mercury were once called *Cynocrambe*, meaning Dog Cabbage.

There should be no problem for the careful forager. The goosefoots tend to have a mealy surface texture on the young leaves at least, while Mercury leaves are very slightly hairy. Dog's Mercury also has underground rhizomes, whereas the goosefoots just have a mass of thin roots. Habitat will also be a reassurance as Dog's Mercury is a plant of shady woods whereas the goosefoots like light and open ground.

Assuming that Annual Mercury *is* poisonous, it presents slightly more of a problem. It often grows in association with other weeds of cultivation – in fact there is a Fat Hen plant clearly visible in the picture on p.178. The long and neatly serrated bright-green leaves are mostly hairless but they also never have that granulated, mealy surface to their young leaves. Remember, it is quite rare outside its stronghold of southern England, so you may not have to worry about it at all.

Henbane *Hyoscyamus niger* xxx

DESCRIPTION	Upright, annual/biennial to 80cm. Single-stemmed. Leaves alternate, deeply toothed edge, hairy, sticky. Stem hairy, sticky. Flowers distinctive, yellow with purple centre. Whole plant smells unpleasant
HABITAT	Disturbed ground, rough agricultural land, coastal dunes
DISTRIBUTION	Uncommon. Southeast England, largely coastal elsewhere
SEASON	May to September

Apart from the common nightshades, such as Black Nightshade and Woody Nightshade, there are several other unpleasant but relatively rare members of the Solanaceae. Their rarity and distinctiveness suggest that they are unlikely to cause you any problems, but it is still important to be aware of them – and they are very pretty too.

Henbane is fairly typical of the nightshades with large berries, flamboyant five-petalled flowers and a generally sinister appearance. Being implicated in the death of Mrs. Crippen, it is also something of a celebrity in the plant world. This association with dastardly deeds long predates Dr Crippen's malfeasance, as we may judge from the eighteenth-century poet William Coombes:

> While whisp'ring Murder tells them that she knows,
> Where the sharp Dagger's forg'd, and Henbane grows.

Despite its murderous reputation, Henbane seldom causes death. But it causes more than its fair share of hair-raising symptoms including thirst, dilated pupils, photophobia, fever, vomiting, accelerated heart rate, hypertension, convulsions, coma and about a dozen more. Hallucinations and euphoria are also among Henbane's extensive arsenal of effects and it is for these that the plant is sometimes, and dangerously, used today.

Pliny the Elder gives us a tip on how Henbane might be so employed: '… *an oil is extracted, which is injected into the ears, and deranges the intellect*'. One wonders how he found this out.

When in flower Henbane is unlikely to confuse anyone as its flowers are so distinctive (pictured overleaf), but the leaves are superficially similar to those of some of the goosefoots, notably Red Goosefoot. Just remember that the latter is hairless, whereas Henbane is covered in long hairs.

Henbane in flower

The closely related and seriously poisonous Thorn Apple (*Datura stramonium*) also has leaves similar to some goosefoots, but they are larger with more pointed, almost holly-like lobes. Also, the flowers are bell-shaped – not spikes of clustered flowers growing from where the leaf joins the stem. Thorn Apple makes the occasional appearance on waste ground and sometimes, unhelpfully, grows in vegetable gardens. It is also known as Jimson Weed after an unfortunate incident in Jamestown involving intoxicated British soldiers during the American War of Independence, and, more tellingly, Loco Weed. Herein lies the main reason why people are poisoned by this plant – its occasional use for 'recreational' purposes. As a fun thing to do at weekends eating Thorn Apple must be near the bottom of the list; the effects are weird, unpredictable and unpleasant, and the chance of killing yourself high. I am going to stick to my Saturday night Ovaltine.

Perhaps the most famous poisonous plant is Deadly Nightshade (*Atropa belladonna*). Nothing about this rare native plant resembles any of the edible species mentioned in this book. Nearly all poisonings from this plant are from children eating the shiny black berries.

P.S. One utterly bizarre use for Henbane from 1657 is in the catching of panthers – animals which, we are told, find Henbane irresistible. Simply hang the plant out of the panther's reach and it '*never leaves off leaping and frisking up and down*' until, exhausted, it '*so dyeth on the place*'.

Black Nightshade *Solanum nigrum* X

DESCRIPTION	Low to medium upright annual, to 60cm. Leaves pointed with rounded base and shallow lobes, hairless or sometimes downy. Flowers white. Berries black
HABITAT	Cultivated ground, waste ground
DISTRIBUTION	Common in England south of Hull, rare in Scotland and Northern Ireland, coastal in Wales
SEASON	Berries July–October

Another very common nightshade, though neither as familiar nor as attractive as Woody Nightshade. Black Nightshade is frequently found in vegetable patches and is often mistaken for a potato plant. Fortunately it does not produce tubers so no harm is done. The young leaves and thoroughly mature berries are not, or at least, not *very*, poisonous and have occasionally been eaten in the past. With so much else to eat I really do not think it is worth the risk.

The immature berries are certainly poisonous, causing headache, diarrhoea and even, very rarely, death due to cardiac and respiratory failure. The toxin is solanine, a glycoalkaloid, which is also known from the skin of poorly stored green potatoes, where it occasionally causes mischief. The mature leaves also contain this toxin and are rather similar to the leaves of some goosefoots, most notably Red Goosefoot. The latter has a mealy coating (little granules) on the young leaves, is hairless and shows a certain amount of red on the mature stems. It also tends to be more of an upright, single-stemmed plant with the leaves forming a rosette and, of course, the flowers are reddish spikes (not five white petals) and the fruit or seeds are inconspicuous – not inside black berries as they are with Black Nightshade.

Woody Nightshade

Solanum dulcamara **XX**

DESCRIPTION	Clambering perennial, up to 2 metres, sometimes forming low sprawling bushes. Leaves pointed with a round base or sometimes a wing, downy. Stems straggling, reddish brown. Flowers have five purple petals folded back with bright-yellow anthers in a column. Berries green, then orange, then red, pointed/oval, hanging down in bunches, usually showing ripe and unripe berries in the same bunch
HABITAT	Hedgerows, on shingle beaches, waste ground
DISTRIBUTION	Very common in England, though less so in the North. Common in central Scotland and the southern half of Northern Ireland
SEASON	Berries May–September

This very familiar plant is also known as Bittersweet owing to the taste of the berries, which is bitter at first then sweet (don't try it). Woody Nightshade is frequently thought to be Deadly Nightshade (*Atropa belladonna*), but they are two distinct, if related, plants. Deadly Nightshade is a fairly rare plant and quite different in appearance, producing single large cherry-like black berries as opposed to Woody Nightshade's clusters of small red berries.

Woody Nightshade is a very beautiful plant with colourful flowers and berries showing all the colours of a traffic light on a single branch. There is little it can be confused with, but is sufficiently common to be worth knowing. There have been poisonings by this plant, usually children attracted by the bright-red berries; flushing of the skin, thirst and abdominal pain are among the symptoms. Normally recovery is complete, but there is one recorded case of a nine-year-old girl who died from internal haemorrhaging after eating them. The level of toxin drops dramatically when the berry is *fully* ripe, presumably to allow birds to distribute the seeds without falling out of the sky. Technically, at this point, one could eat them but this, of course, is a prime example of 'don't try this at home'.

Foxglove *Digitalis purpurea* XXX

DESCRIPTION	Tall, upright perennial, to 1.5 metres. Thick, soft, furry leaves arranged around a central stem. Flowers a distinctive purple/pink bell shape, in a tall spike
HABITAT	Woods, scrub, hedgerows and heath
DISTRIBUTION	Very common throughout the UK, save the Fens
SEASON	Flowers June–September. Leaves much of the year

No visitor to the countryside in high summer will have failed to notice this handsome plant; it graces many of our roadsides and fills many woodland clearings, buzzing with its attendant bees. In full bloom no one could mistake this plant for anything else, but the leaves are rather similar to those of Comfrey, a plant which is sometimes eaten (see below). Should, as has happened, any such mistake be made it is going to be a big one as this plant is utterly deadly.

The poison is a group of chemicals generically called digitalin, which affects the heart and is deadly in even tiny doses – 10mg (one fiftieth of the weight of a single paracetamol tablet) is invariably fatal. This quantity is easily contained in one or two leaves and it was two leaves that, sadly, an amateur botanist used recently to end his life, carefully avoiding a larger dose which would have caused vomiting.

P.S. The father of modern pharmacology is the admirable doctor, botanist and chemist, William Withering. In 1775 he learned from an old woman (some say, romantically, that she was a gypsy) a remedy for the oedema caused by heart failure, better known then as dropsy. The mixture consisted of twenty herbs, but Withering managed to settle on Foxglove as being the active ingredient. To his great credit he then proceeded to carefully measure its effect in differing doses (starting with a very low dose) on 163 patients. He recorded his results, publishing them *whether or not* they supported his tentative contention that the herb was of use in curing dropsy. This thoughtful and systematic procedure was a major break with the superstitious guesswork of the past and marks the birth of true medical research.

Before Wittering, Foxgloves had been considered to have little application in herbal medicine. Gerard talks of them being '*of no use, neither have they any place amongst medicines*', and Culpeper unenthusiastically lists a dozen ailments that Foxgloves might alleviate, none of which is dropsy. Digoxin and digitoxin are now extremely important drugs, strengthening and slowing the heart beat, but dosage is extremely critical and one may forgive the old herbalists for wanting little to do with the plant that contains them. In medicine there is something called the therapeutic index, which, crudely put, is the ratio between the dose that will cure you and the dose that will kill you (or at least do considerable harm). A comfortable index is about 100 – with digitalin it is around 2 or 3.

Withering himself died young at the age of 58, probably from consumption. As he lay dying a friend wrote, in a remarkable congruence of wit, admiration and tactlessness, 'The flower of English botany is Withering.'

P.P.S. Comfrey, the plant that Foxglove is sometimes confused with, has long been considered an edible plant, albeit not a particularly popular one. It has also been used for centuries in herbal remedies – internally for a variety of ailments and, more usefully, externally as a poultice of the leaves or roots to aid the healing of sprains, burns and broken bones. This latter use is reflected in the Latin name *Symphytum* which means 'to make whole'.

Unfortunately a dark suspicion has fallen on Comfrey and it is now considered to be quite seriously poisonous, causing dangerous liver conditions and even liver cancer. In 2001, the US Food and Drugs Administration banned its use in herbal preparations, expressing serious concern over the plant's safety and citing a number of incidents of disease and at least one death. Cirrhosis and veno-occlusion (blockage) of the liver are the main problems. Only after a considerable amount has been consumed over a period of months do the cumulative effects of the highly poisonous pyrrolizidine alkaloids manifest themselves. The roots, which have occasionally been consumed as a vegetable, contain large quantities of the toxins and young leaves relatively small amounts. The mature leaves contain less still.

It could be argued that the occasional Comfrey fritter made from older leaves would do little harm, but the Velcro texture never completely disappears and I don't think that the forager will lose a great deal by banishing Comfrey from the menu.

Lords and Ladies *Arum maculatum* X

DESCRIPTION	Short perennial, to 40cm. Leaves large, arrow-shaped, stemmed, often spotted. Flowers a single brown club enclosed in a large open sheath. Berries clustered on a spike, red
HABITAT	Woods, hedgerows, copses. Shade-loving
DISTRIBUTION	Very common throughout the British Isles, except central Wales and the Scottish Highlands
SEASON	Leaves January–May, Flowers April–June, berries May –September

The leaves of Lords and Ladies often dominate the woodland and hedgerow of late winter and early spring, and will persist for several months before the plant transforms itself into the second of its three manifestations. It is this stage, the flowering stage, that gives the plant a fair proportion of its one hundred or so common names.

Lords and Ladies is a coy reference to the impressively vertical central spadix resting in its sheath-like spathe. Another familiar name is Cuckoo Pint. The Cuckoo part is either derived from 'cuckold' or a reference to the energetic behaviour of the male cuckoo. Pint is clear enough, being shortened from 'pintle'; the Wiltshire name

A spike of Lords and Ladies berries

Dog Cock puts it more straightforwardly. Incidentally 'Pint' should be pronounced to rhyme with 'mint'. My favourite piece of rural circumlocution is Wake Robin – 'Robin' is an affectionate name similar to Dick or John Thomas and 'Wake' just tells you what mood he is in. Like all good things, this flowering stage eventually passes to be replaced by the berries on a spike.

The leaves of Lords and Ladies are not terribly poisonous, acting mostly as an irritant. However, they do have the potentially serious effect of swelling up the tongue and throat. As an inveterate nibbler of wild plants (worth doing only if you are *very* careful and are familiar with the dangerous plants), I once tried the tiniest piece of Lords and Ladies, spitting out as much as I could after a few seconds. The tip of my tongue went numb and my lips swelled as though I had been using lip-plumping lipstick (not that I would know). After a few minutes my whole throat and oesophagus started to feel on fire. It is for this reason that the plant seldom causes problems – few can eat enough to poison themselves.

The main potential for confusion is with Sorrel. The two plants are completely unrelated, but the leaves sometimes look worryingly similar. There are many differences but the easy one, if you are in doubt, is that the backward-pointing lobes of Sorrel are always sharply pointed, whereas those of Lords and Ladies are slightly rounded. A few of the goosefoots have arrow-shaped leaves, but they always grow from a central stem and will often have a granular surface, especially when young.

The berries are the most poisonous part of Lords and Ladies, but their growth habit as solitary spikes is unlike that of any edible plant – only children or the foolhardy are ever poisoned.

Sorrel above, Lords and Ladies below

Black Bryony

White Bryony

Black Bryony *Tamus communis* xx

DESCRIPTION	Perennial climber, up to 4 metres long. Leaves distinctly heart-shaped, light green. Flowers small, pale yellow/green, six-petalled. Bright-red berries appear, along with the immature yellow and green ones, in long strings
HABITAT	Woods, hedgerows, scrub
DISTRIBUTION	Very common in England, except the North. Rare in central Wales, absent elsewhere
SEASON	Berries September–November

The bright-red, yellow and green strings of Black Bryony berries festoon the autumn hedgerow like early Christmas decorations. They are larger in size than most hedgerow berries and do look quite tasty, but their colourful 'pearl necklace' growth habit makes them very easily distinguishable from the edible berries. Black Bryony is quite poisonous, the commonest effect being an irritation of the skin and mouth caused by tiny needles of calcium oxalate penetrating the skin. The berries also contain irritant histamines and bitter saponins.

Black Bryony is unusual in being the only member in the British Isles of the otherwise exotic yam family. Another bryony, much less common than Black Bryony and totally unrelated to it, is White Bryony (*Bryonia dioica*). This, too, is the only wild British representative of its family, the cucumbers. It is also seriously poisonous and grows as a climber. Its leaves are maple-like and it clings to the hedgerow with spiralling tendrils. It produces clusters of poisonous red berries.

Yew *Taxus baccata* xxx

DESCRIPTION	Large tree. Needles in opposing rows. Berries bright scarlet
HABITAT	Frequently planted, often on lime. Churchyards, old gardens
DISTRIBUTION	Very common; uncommon or missing in northern Scotland and Northern Ireland
SEASON	Berries September and October

I cannot really imagine anyone eating any part of the splendid Yew by mistake, but it certainly has happened. The most usual victims are children, attracted by the bright berries – they do look rather tasty and a woman in Germany in 1975 unaccountably ate four or five handfuls of leaves and duly died. In fact nearly all parts of the Yew are seriously poisonous and often deadly, containing as they do the chemical *taxin,* which interferes with heart action. The one exception is the soft part of the fruit. This means that you can eat the berries as long as you spit out the pips without chewing them. Obviously I have tried them and find them to be slightly mucilaginous and pleasantly sweet, though not very fruity. I suppose a jelly could be made out of it, or perhaps a sorbet for an extreme dinner party. Maybe not.

P.S. The Yew is one of only three native British conifers, the others being Juniper and Scots Pine. Since they are all conifers one is entitled to expect them all to bear cones. The cones of Scots Pine are quite obvious but the other two appear to have berries instead. However, if you look closely at a Juniper berry you can see that it is a tiny, soft pine cone. But what of the Yew? In fact the red fleshy part of the berry – the aril – is a highly modified cone scale. If you look at the immature berry it actually looks like a tiny acorn.

Recipes

Nettle soup

Nettle Soup is probably what most people first think of when they consider cooking on the wild side, so I could hardly leave it out. The keys to an excellent Nettle Soup are potato – to give it body – and really good stock – to give it spirit. Without these the wild food cynic's worst suspicions of boiled weeds will be confirmed. Note that a carrier bag is the standard measure for Nettles.

Serves 4

Half a carrier bagful of Stinging Nettle tops, or fresh-looking larger leaves
50g butter
1 large onion (or a dozen Crow Garlic bulbs if you want to be truly wild), peeled and finely chopped
1 litre vegetable or chicken stock, or even light fish stock
1 large potato, peeled and cut into cubes
1 large carrot, peeled and chopped
Sea salt and freshly ground black pepper
2 tbsp crème fraîche
A few drops of extra-virgin olive oil
A few drops of Tabasco

Wearing rubber gloves, sort through the Nettles, discarding anything you don't like the look of and any thick stalks. Wash the Nettles and drain in a colander.

Melt the butter in a large saucepan, add the onion and cook gently for 5–7 minutes until softened. Add the stock, Nettles, potato and carrot. Bring to a simmer and cook gently until the potato is soft, about 15 minutes. Remove from the heat.

Using an electric hand-held stick blender, purée the soup and then season with salt and pepper to taste.

Ladle into warmed bowls and float a teaspoonful of crème fraîche on top. As this melts, swirl in a few drops of extra-virgin olive oil and Tabasco.

Hogweed tempura

There is something incongruous about this name, a bit like 'Winkles Beurre Meunière'. 'Hogweed in Batter' would be a little more straightforward but just doesn't sound the same and, of course, it isn't the same. Japanese tempura is on a higher plane than humble batter and once you have mastered the necessary oriental incantations is very easy to make.

Before you embark on those incantations do make sure to read the chapter on picking Hogweed shoots – it has some very dangerous look-alikes.

Serves 4

200ml lager or light beer
12–16 young Hogweed shoots
Sunflower oil, for deep-frying
50g plain flour
50g cornflour
½ tsp salt

For the dipping sauce
2 tbsp soy sauce
2 tbsp mirin (rice wine)
1 level tsp sesame seeds

Put the lager in the fridge (or in the freezer as long as you can trust yourself not to leave it there for longer than 30 minutes). Rinse the Hogweed shoots, drain and pat dry. Mix together the ingredients for the dipping sauce in a serving bowl.

Heat the oil in a suitable deep, heavy pan until it registers 180°C on a frying thermometer. Meanwhile, mix the flour, cornflour and salt together in a bowl and make a well in the middle. Just before the oil reaches the required temperature, pour the lager into the flour and mix to a batter *very quickly and leaving in lots of lumps*.

Immediately dip a batch of the Hogweed shoots into the batter, shaking off the excess and quickly lower them, one at a time, into the hot oil. The cooking time is very brief at only a minute, or possibly two for any thicker pieces.

Drain the cooked Hogweed pieces on kitchen paper to absorb the excess oil; keep hot. Use a slotted spoon to remove any stray bits of batter in the oil before cooking the next batch. Eat while hot, with the dipping sauce.

Wild stir-fry

This is a spring recipe for the purist – everything in it is wild. Well, everything except the oil. The only thing in this book that contains any quantity of oil is Hazelnut, but unless you have a three-ton oil press to hand, there is no sensible way of getting to it. I have come to terms with this small failing.

Rather than restricting the stir-fry to plants, I have introduced wild foods from my other River Cottage Handbooks: *Edible Seashore* and *Mushrooms*.

Serves 2

2 or 3 Bulrush shoots, washed
Handful of dulse, washed
Handful of Jelly Ears (if you can find some), cleaned
1 tbsp pepper dulse, washed

About 10 Crow Garlic bulbs, peeled
Handful of Sea Beet leaves or shoots
1 tbsp good-quality oil
2 tsp seawater

Remove the tougher outer leaves of the Bulrush shoots, then cut into 1cm lengths. Slice the dulse and the Jelly Ears into strips. Finely chop the pepper dulse and the Crow Garlic. The Sea Beet leaves or shoots should be left whole, unless they are particularly large.

Warm the oil with the seawater in a wok or large frying pan. Add the dulse, Crow Garlic and Jelly Ears, cover and simmer gently for 5 minutes. Remove the lid, add the remaining ingredients and turn up the heat. Stir-fry for 3 minutes, then serve in warmed bowls.

Wild Garlic parcels

Wild Garlic Parcels are a decidedly temperate-zone take on the Greek dolma – the stuffed vine leaves of many a sunshine holiday. This is a meaty version, but the sausage could easily be replaced with vegetables.

Serves 4

32 large young Wild Garlic leaves
100g arborio rice, cooked
250g sausagemeat (or black
   pudding, or a mixture of both)

200ml good chicken or vegetable
   stock
Sea salt and freshly ground black
   pepper

Preheat the oven to 190°C/Gas mark 5. Clean the Wild Garlic leaves, separate the stalks and chop these finely. In a bowl, mix the chopped garlic stalks with the rice, sausagemeat and some salt and pepper. Lay the Wild Garlic leaves shiny side down on a board, in pairs to form a cross. Place a teaspoonful of the rice mixture on the centre of the cross then, starting with the bottommost leaf, wrap them around to form little parcels. Turn the parcels over and place in a baking dish. Pour the stock over them, then cover with a lid or foil and bake for 45 minutes.

Wild Garlic pesto

Wild Garlic lends itself perfectly to a pesto and Pignuts make an excellent wild replacement for the familiar pine nuts.

Makes 1 small jar

50g Wild Garlic leaves, washed
30g Pignuts, sliced and briefly
    toasted in a little oil in a frying pan,
    then chopped

30g Parmesan cheese, freshly grated
80ml olive oil, plus extra to cover
Sea salt and freshly ground black
    pepper

The simplest method is to put everything except the oil in a food processor, blitz for a few seconds, then continue to whiz while slowly adding the olive oil through the funnel. I prefer to leave things a little coarser and take the traditional path of finely chopping the Wild Garlic leaves, then grinding them with the Pignuts, Parmesan and seasoning, using a large pestle and mortar, and adding the olive oil towards the end. Whichever you decide upon, transfer to a jar, pour sufficient olive oil on top to keep the pesto covered, close the lid and store it in the fridge. Under its layer of oil, the pesto will keep for several weeks.

Nettle ravioli

These look magnificent and will convince everyone of your wild foody credentials. Years ago, I watched my friend Rosanna, a Neapolitan mamma of classic proportions and character, rolling out pasta sheets and cutting tagliatelle with the expertise that came from a lifetime's experience. For mortals, a cheap pasta-making machine is a safer route to take. Making your own pasta with one of these is fun and not at all difficult, unless your machine has more personality than is good for it. The commonest type has little scrapers underneath the rollers designed to remove errant pieces of pasta that get stuck. Unfortunately these bend easily and the machine becomes bunged up with pasta. We are only allotted a certain amount of patience and mine ran out about twenty years ago, so I removed these useless pieces of metal with a pair of pliers. I haven't looked back. Apart from this necessary piece of engineering, the real key to keeping everything moving is to scatter flour about the place as though you are not the one who will have to clear it up later.

Serves 4

For the pasta
100g Stinging Nettle leaves
500g Italian '00' pasta flour
4 large eggs
½ tsp sea salt

For the filling
50g Stinging Nettle leaves
25g Pignuts, plus a little oil (or Hazelnuts or pine kernels)

25g Wild Garlic leaves (or an ordinary garlic clove)
1 egg
Sea salt and freshly ground black pepper

To serve
Melted butter, freshly grated Parmesan or Wild Garlic Pesto (p. 205)

Wash the Nettles (for the pasta and filling), simmer in a little water for 10 minutes, then drain thoroughly. For the pasta, take two-thirds of the Nettles and squeeze out as much water as you can, then chop them very, very finely, almost to a powder.

Heap the flour into a mound on a clean surface, make a well in the middle and add the eggs and salt. Start to mix to a dough, then add the Nettles and continue kneading until it is an even green colour. The dough should be quite firm; if it gets too sticky, sprinkle on a little flour; if too dry, knead in a little water. Wrap in cling film and refrigerate for 20 minutes.

Meanwhile, make the filling. Slice the Pignuts and briefly sauté in a little oil (or just chop other nuts). Chop the remaining (cooked) Nettles and the Wild Garlic (just crush ordinary garlic). In a bowl, mix the Nettles, Pignuts, Wild Garlic and egg together and season with salt and pepper to taste.

Roll out the pasta into thin sheets, using a pasta machine; keep the sheets covered with a very slightly damp tea-towel as you work, to prevent them drying out.

One sheet at a time, cut out rounds, using a 6cm pastry cutter. Spoon a little of the filling into the centre of half of the pasta discs and place another disc on top of each. Press firmly with a ravioli press (if you have one) or just press the edges together firmly and crimp with the handle of a knife. Keep covered while making the rest.

Bring a large pan of salted water to a rolling boil. Add the ravioli and cook at a fast boil until *al dente* (tender but firm to the bite), about 3–4 minutes. Drain thoroughly and serve on warmed plates, topped with melted butter or grated Parmesan or, best of all, with Wild Garlic Pesto.

Watercress omelette with
cream cheese and smoked salmon

Despite looking uncannily like a certain variety of foam-rubber carpet underlay, this is a rather delicious soufflé omelette. The whisking and folding of the egg whites is a labour of love but it does make a lighter omelette. Just about everything could be changed if you want – the Watercress could easily be Chickweed, Fat Hen or several of the other wild greens in this book and the filling could be just about anything you fancy.

Makes 2 (each serves 1 generously or 2)

85g Watercress, washed
4 eggs, separated
2 tbsp crème fraîche
Sea salt and freshly ground black
  pepper
A little oil for cooking

For the filling
75g cream cheese
100g smoked salmon slices
Handful of Sorrel leaves, washed and
  shredded (optional)

Blitz the Watercress, egg yolks, crème fraîche and some salt and pepper together in a blender for a few seconds.

Beat the egg whites in a scrupulously clean bowl with a balloon whisk until they form soft peaks, then carefully fold into the Watercress mixture.

Heat a little oil in a medium frying pan and pour in half of the omelette mixture. Cook for a couple of minutes until set and golden brown underneath, then carefully transfer to a warmed plate. Repeat to cook the second omelette.

Top with the cream cheese and smoked salmon and sprinkle with shredded Sorrel if you have some to hand. Fold to enclose the filling and eat straight away.

Chickweed pakoras

The slightly stringy nature of Chickweed can make it something of a trial in the kitchen and Pakoras are by far the best way to use it. This is a difficult recipe to get wrong – almost any quantities of the various ingredients will work – just make sure you use plenty of salt. The tablespoonful of medium-hot curry powder I suggest gives a mild flavour with a little warmth; if you like it hot then up the quantity or use a hotter powder. There may be purists who baulk at the idea of ready-made curry powder; if you are one, then feel free to use coriander, cumin, turmeric, chilli and so on – in whatever proportions you like.

Fat Hen, Sea Beet and several other green leaves in this book will work just as well in this incredibly quick, cheap and delicious recipe.

Makes 8

100g gram (chickpea) flour
1 tbsp medium curry powder, or to taste
½ tsp baking powder
½ tsp sea salt (or more)
About 120ml water

50g Chickweed, washed, dried and roughly chopped
10 Crow Garlic bulbs, or 1 small onion and 1 ordinary garlic clove, peeled and finely chopped
Vegetable oil for shallow-frying

Mix the flour, curry powder, baking powder and salt together in a bowl, then slowly stir in enough water to form a paste the consistency of mustard. Mix in the Chickweed and Crow Garlic and stir until they are well coated in the paste.

Heat a thin layer of oil in a heavy-based frying pan. When hot, spoon in heaped dessertspoonfuls of the pakora mixture to form little cakes, spacing them well apart. Cover with a lid and cook over a medium heat for about 5 minutes until crisp and golden brown on one side. Turn the cakes over to brown the other side. Drain on kitchen paper and serve at once.

Sorrel and Fat Hen tart

This is a substantial and delicious tart recipe, which allows for an endless variety of fillings. It would be particularly good with Sorrel and Hop tops.

Serves 6–8

For the pastry
200g plain flour
A pinch of salt
100g cold, unsalted butter, cut into
  small cubes
1 egg, separated
About 50ml cold milk

For the filling
A knob of unsalted butter
1 onion, peeled and finely sliced
30g Sorrel, washed
70g Fat Hen, Watercress or
  Stinging Nettles, washed
200g goat's cheese
3 eggs, plus 2 egg yolks
200ml double cream
Sea salt and freshly ground black pepper

To make the pastry, put the flour, salt and butter into a food processor and pulse until the mixture resembles breadcrumbs. Add the egg yolks and then, with the motor running, trickle in the milk through the funnel, stopping the moment the dough comes together. Tip on to a lightly floured surface and knead gently to make a smooth ball. Wrap in cling film and rest in the fridge for 30 minutes.

Preheat the oven to 170°C/Gas mark 3. Roll out the pastry on a lightly floured surface and use to line a 28cm loose-bottomed tart tin, allowing the excess pastry to overhang the rim of the tin. Rest in the fridge for 20 minutes.

Prick the pastry base with a fork. Line with a sheet of greaseproof paper and fill with baking beans or rice. Bake for 15 minutes, then remove the paper and beans and return to the oven for 10 minutes until the base looks dry and cooked. Lightly beat the egg white and brush all over the pastry to seal, then bake for a further 5 minutes until golden. Trim off the excess pastry from the edge with a small, sharp knife.

For the filling, heat the butter in a frying pan over a low heat, add the onion and fry very gently until soft and pale golden, about 15 minutes. Remove from the heat. Roughly chop the Sorrel and Fat Hen and wilt in a steamer for 2–3 minutes. Scatter the wilted greens and onions evenly in the pastry case, then crumble over the goat's cheese. Whisk together the whole eggs, egg yolks and cream with some salt and pepper and carefully pour over the filling.

Bake for 40 minutes until the filling is lightly set and browned. Serve warm or cold.

Juniper pot

The extremely rich nature of this unusual dish is cut back nicely by the Juniper berries and by the lactic acid in the crème fraîche. I am grateful to my friend Helle for passing on this Danish triumph. This is one of the few savoury dishes I know that contains neither onions nor garlic.

Serves 2

500g pork loin
8 Juniper berries (or more if you
   really love the flavour)
Leaves from 1 rosemary twig
20g butter

125ml single cream (or more if you
   like lots of sauce for your mash)
125ml crème fraîche
Sea salt and freshly ground black
   pepper

Trim any excess fat from the pork, then cut into small steaks. Crush the Juniper berries and rosemary using a pestle and mortar.

Heat the butter in a wide heavy-based saucepan. Add the meat and brown lightly on both sides. Stir in the cream, crème fraîche and some salt and pepper. Place the lid on the pan and cook on a very low heat (at a bare simmer) for 1 hour, stirring occasionally. If it appears too dry, then stir in a little more cream.

Serve with mashed potato or rice and a green vegetable.

Hen chicken

Basing a recipe on word play is not necessarily a good idea but works quite nicely on this occasion. It is a pretty straightforward recipe with a reassuringly short list of ingredients – only the stuffing of the chicken breasts presents anything in the way of a challenge.

Serves 4

200g Fat Hen (or any other wild green vegetable that tastes good when cooked), washed
30g Wild Garlic leaves, washed
20g butter
4 large free-range chicken breasts, boned and skinned
100g streaky bacon rashers
300ml good-quality chicken stock
Sea salt and freshly ground black pepper

Preheat the oven to 190°C/Gas mark 5. Coarsely chop the Fat Hen and Wild Garlic. Sweat them together with the butter in a covered frying pan for 5 minutes, adding a splash of water to prevent sticking. Season with salt and pepper to taste. Allow to cool, then squeeze out excess water.

Here is the technical bit. A chicken breast is made up of two muscles – one large, one small. Carefully cut them apart. Take the larger piece, hold it flat on a board with the palm of your hand and, using a really sharp knife held horizontally, cut a pocket in the meat. Stuff the pocket with a quarter of the cooked greens, then place the smaller fillet over the gap. Wrap with a single layer of streaky bacon. Repeat for the other three breasts.

Lay the stuffed chicken breasts in a baking dish (with lid), season with salt and pepper and pour over the stock. Put the lid on and place in the oven. Cook for 20 minutes, basting at least twice, then remove the lid and continue to cook for a further 20–30 minutes depending on size, until the chicken is cooked right through and the bacon is slightly crisp.

Transfer the chicken breasts to warm plates and pour over the cooking juices. (If the stock is a little too thin, bubble vigorously to reduce before pouring over the chicken.) Serve with rice or new potatoes and a green vegetable.

Beef casserole with Horseradish and Chestnut dumplings

Horseradish is almost invariably used to make a sauce and is seldom cooked. The hot taste so appreciated with roast beef normally disappears during cooking, but the gentle and fairly brief cooking it receives here ensures a certain amount of bite is retained – but not too much. The Chestnuts add richness and sweetness, helping to make these the best dumplings I have ever tasted. The basic beef casserole is slightly stolen from Hugh's *River Cottage Meat Book*. I am sure he won't mind.

Serves 4

25g butter
250g onions, peeled and chopped
125g salt pork, pancetta or bacon off-cuts, cut into smaller chunks
750g boneless shin of beef or other stewing beef, cut into chunks
25g plain flour, sifted
500ml stout or beef stock (or any combination of the two)
2 bay leaves
1 tsp thyme leaves

For the dumplings
75g self-raising flour
25g Chestnut flour
A pinch of baking powder
50g freshly grated Horseradish
50g shredded suet
About 75ml water
Sea salt and freshly ground black pepper

Preheat the oven to 120°C/Gas mark ½. Heat the butter in a large frying pan. Add the onions with the pork or bacon and brown lightly, then transfer to a casserole dish with a slotted spoon, leaving the fat in the pan. Now brown the beef, in batches, in the pan. Once it is all browned, return the beef to the pan, sprinkle on the flour and stir to mix with and thicken the juices. Transfer the beef to the casserole dish.

Pour the stock/stout into the frying pan, stirring to mix with the sediment, then pour into the casserole dish. Add the herbs and some salt and pepper. Cover and cook in the oven for 2¾ hours if using shin, otherwise 2¼ hours, stirring occasionally. If necessary, add a little water halfway through cooking to keep the meat moist.

Meanwhile, make the dumplings. Mix the flours, baking powder, Horseradish and suet together in a bowl, then incorporate enough water to make a soft dough. Knead lightly and shape into balls, about 3cm in diameter.

Take out the casserole and sit the dumplings on top of the stew. Put the lid back on and return to the oven for a further 25 minutes or until the dumplings are cooked.

Watermint sorbet

This is one of the lightest and most refreshing desserts there is. Lemon sorbet is sometimes used to restore the palate between courses and this is even better. Interestingly – well, I think it's interesting – sometimes it comes out pale pink and sometimes pale green – it all seems to depend on the infusion temperature and when you add the lemon juice. Unfortunately I have never quite worked out the details and the colour always comes as a surprise.

The best alternative to Watermint is Elderflower, but it also works nicely with Japanese Rose or Spearmint.

Serves 6

650g caster sugar
800ml water
Juice of 4 lemons

Small handful (about 20g) Watermint, plus a few nice sprigs to finish

Put the sugar and water into a large saucepan and heat gently, stirring to dissolve the sugar, then add the lemon juice and Watermint. Set aside to cool, then pass the infused sugar syrup through a fine sieve to strain out the Watermint.

Churn the sugar syrup in an ice-cream machine until very thick, then transfer to the freezer to set firm (unless serving straight away). If you do not have an ice-cream maker, then put the mixture into a shallow container and place in the freezer until it is nearly frozen but still with some liquid. Take it out, crush into manageable chunks with the end of a rolling pin and whiz in a blender to break down the ice crystals, then return to the container and freeze. Do this a couple more times until a consistent, smooth sorbet is formed.

This dessert is certainly best served soon after making, but if you store it in the freezer for a while, take it out 10–15 minutes before serving to allow it to soften. Serve in glass dishes, topped with Watermint sprigs.

Bramble mousse

I am most grateful to my friend Pam Corbin for this substantial recipe. Blackberry picking is gruelling, exacting and dangerous work, so you deserve the best reward for your labours. Here it is.

Serves 4

500g Blackberries, washed
7g leaf gelatine
Juice of ½ lemon (omit if your
   Blackberries are strongly acidic)

3 large eggs
100g caster sugar
200ml double cream

Set aside 50g of the best Blackberries for serving. Put the rest into a saucepan, cover and cook gently for 5 minutes until softened. Meanwhile, soak the gelatine leaves in a shallow dish of cold water to soften.

Crush the cooked Blackberries in the saucepan using a potato masher, then pass through a sieve into a bowl, pressing with the back of a wooden spoon to extract as much juice as possible. If you want to get every last drop of juice out (and you should), squeeze the pulp left in the sieve in a muslin bag. Rinse out the saucepan.

Pour the Blackberry juice into the pan, add the lemon juice and heat gently until almost simmering, then take off the heat. Squeeze the gelatine leaves to remove excess water, then add them to the hot blackberry juice and stir until dissolved. Set aside to cool until tepid.

In a large bowl, whisk the eggs with the caster sugar until thick, pale and mousse-like. Continuing to whisk, slowly pour in the Blackberry juice, followed by 150ml of the cream.

Pour the mixture into glasses and place in the fridge for a couple of hours until set. Before serving, pour a little cream on top and decorate with the remaining berries.

Cranberry and apple tart

The Cranberries on this tart were hard won on a trip to a remote Scottish bog and I wanted to make the most of them. Thankfully Pam Corbin came up with a recipe that would show the berries in all their glory. If you cannot afford the time to wander hopefully around northern bogs then almost any autumn fruit will do. Bilberry is an obvious alternative, but Blackberries would look great too.

Serves 6

For the Hazelnut pastry
30g shelled Hazelnuts
175g plain flour
100g butter, cut into small cubes
50g caster sugar
1 egg, beaten

For the filling
500g cooking apples
25g butter
50ml water
50g sugar
50–75g Cranberries
8–10 Crab Apples
Juice of ½ lemon
Caster sugar for sprinkling

Preheat the oven to 200°C/Gas mark 6. Scatter the Hazelnuts on a baking tray and toast in the oven for about 5 minutes. Chop the nuts very finely or blitz in a food processor. Put the flour into a large bowl, add the butter and rub in until the mixture resembles fine breadcrumbs. Stir in the sugar and Hazelnuts. Finally, mix in the egg to form a smooth dough. Wrap in cling film and rest in the fridge for 30 minutes.

Peel, core and roughly chop the cooking apples and place them in a saucepan with the butter and water. Cover and cook gently until the apples are soft and fluffy. Stir in the sugar and half of the Cranberries (less if you do not have many).

Roll out the pastry on a lightly floured surface and use to line an 18–20cm flan tin. Prick the base lightly. Line the pastry case with greaseproof paper and baking beans or rice and bake for 15 minutes. Remove the paper and beans or rice and return the flan to the oven for 5 minutes to dry and cook the base. Let cool slightly.

Spread the apple and Cranberry filling in the pastry case. Finely slice the Crab Apples crossways, pushing the pips out to reveal a star-shaped pattern. Toss the slices in the lemon juice to stop them browning. Arrange the Crab Apple slices around the edge of the tart and sprinkle them with a little caster sugar. Return the tart to the oven for 15–20 minutes until the Crab Apple discs are cooked. Place the tin on a wire rack and allow to cool. Pile the remaining Cranberries in the centre of the tart to serve.

Rosehip babas with Blackberries

In the early 1970s I spent a few unsettling months living in the Tahiti Hotel in Aldershot. It was not a nice place to live. The kitchen facilities mercifully did not exist so I ate out every day in any one of Aldershot's many fine cafes. My diet consisted almost entirely of egg, sausage, chips and babas. Rum babas were popular at the time but have now fallen out of favour; perhaps it is the fabulous number of calories they provide. I would like to see them back, just for old times' sake.

Ideally, you need to get hold of the special baba tins, although mini flan dishes may just fit the bill.

Makes 6

7g sachet dried yeast
75ml warm milk
1 tbsp caster sugar
125g plain flour
2 large eggs
75g unsalted butter, softened

For the syrup
150ml home-made Rosehip Syrup
  (p.91)
100ml rum or brandy

To serve
200g Blackberries
150ml single cream

Mix the yeast, warm milk and sugar together in a large bowl and leave in a warm place for 15 minutes until it starts to froth. Butter six individual baba tins.

Add the flour and eggs to the yeast mixture and beat thoroughly with a spoon. Add the softened butter and continue to stir until you have a smooth mixture.

Half fill your baba tins with the mixture and leave the tins in a warm place until the mixture has risen to the top of the tins. Preheat the oven to 180°C/Gas mark 4.

Bake the babas for 20–25 minutes until golden. They are rather unforgiving when it comes to cooking times; the difference between undercooked and slightly burnt is about 2 minutes! Leave to cool a little on a wire rack, then carefully remove from their tins – not the easiest of manoeuvres, but using a thin plastic knife will help.

While the babas are still slightly warm, mix the Rosehip Syrup and rum or brandy together and pour over the babas. Fill with Blackberries and serve with cream.

Chestnut pancakes with
Birch Sap Syrup

It is always good to have more than one wild foraged ingredient in a recipe and to put two distinctly woodland foods together is particularly satisfying. Of course you can substitute home-made Chestnut flour with a commercial one, or Birch Sap Syrup with imported maple syrup if you need to. This is one of the simplest recipes in the book, with the plain wheat flour of an ordinary pancake being replaced with Chestnut flour. The flavour is fairly intense and complex, and also quite sweet, so that only a small amount of syrup will be needed.

Before we start, here is an easy way to make Chestnut flour: Place the Chestnuts in a pan of cold water and bring to the boil. Cook gently for 10 minutes, or 15 minutes if they are large. Turn off the heat, but leave the Chestnuts in the hot water. Don a pair of rubber gloves. One at a time, remove the Chestnuts, cut into the pointed end on the flat side and start to peel the skin. Usually, both layers come away together.

Cool the peeled Chestnuts in the fridge, then grate them in a Mouli grater. Spread thinly on a non-stick baking tray and place in a very low oven (40°C), with the door slightly ajar, for an hour or until perfectly dry. Blitz the dried Chestnut flakes in a blender to a powder. The result will not be as fine as wheat flour but this does not matter, not a bit.

Serves 2

2 eggs	Sunflower or corn oil, for frying
100g Chestnut flour	Birch Sap Syrup (p.161) or Wild
250ml milk	Flower Syrup (p.237)

Crack the eggs into a bowl, add the flour and mix to a paste. Slowly add the milk, stirring all the time to prevent it going lumpy. Alternatively (and much easier), put all three ingredients into the bowl at the same time and mix with an electric hand-held stick blender. Leave the batter to stand for an hour.

Heat a little oil in a small non-stick frying pan. Stir the pancake batter, then pour or spoon in enough to thinly cover the base of the pan or, if you want interesting shapes (like those in the picture), a little less.

When the top surface takes on a translucent appearance, turn the pancake over and cook the other side for a minute or two. Repeat with the rest of the batter. Serve immediately, with a small quantity of syrup trickled over.

Chestnut Florentines

As you may have noticed I have become a bit of a Chestnut flour bore, insisting that everyone puts it into every conceivable recipe. Certainly if you want your sauces, cakes, dumplings or biscuits to be sweeter and richer there is no better way. Commercially bought Chestnut flour is very expensive, but the forager laughs at such things – his or her Chestnut flour costs nothing. To make it, see the recipe for Chestnut Pancakes (p.226).

Makes about 10

50g butter
50g caster sugar
50g honey
25g Chestnut flour
40g shelled Hazelnuts, coarsely
  crushed

2 tsp double cream
About 20 Rosehips, carefully
  seeded and coarsely chopped

To finish (optional)
About 40g dark chocolate

Preheat the oven to 170°C/Gas mark 3. Line a large baking tray with baking parchment.

Put the butter, sugar and honey in a small saucepan and heat gently until everything has melted. Turn off the heat and stir in the Chestnut flour, crushed Hazelnuts, cream and chopped Rosehips until evenly combined.

Using a dessertspoon, drop small mounds of the mixture on to the prepared baking tray, leaving plenty of space in between to allow for spreading. Bake in the oven for 8–10 minutes until golden. Leave the Florentines to firm up on the baking tray until almost cold, then carefully lift off on to a wire rack.

I think these are lovely just as they are, but if you like you can melt the chocolate in a bain-marie (or heatproof bowl over a pan of simmering water) and use to carefully coat the bottom of each Florentine; place them upside down on a wire rack to set. This can be a messy business, but there are worse things.

Chestnut macaroons

Chestnut flour can be a difficult ingredient in bread and cakes, refusing to allow them to rise in quite the way the cook would like. In this recipe, however, it behaves better than the ground almond it replaces, making perfectly formed macaroons every time.

Makes about 8

100g Chestnut flour (p.226)
20g rice flour
200g caster sugar

2 large egg whites
25g shelled Hazelnuts, coarsely
   chopped

Preheat the oven to 170°C/Gas mark 3. Line a large baking tray with rice paper (which is usually made from potatoes, by the way).

Mix the Chestnut flour, rice flour and sugar together in a bowl. Beat the egg white lightly (don't worry if it is not perfectly frothy) and stir into the mixture.

Drop heaped dessertspoonfuls of the mixture on to the prepared baking tray, spacing them well apart. Sprinkle the chopped Hazelnuts on top. Bake in the oven for 20–25 minutes until golden brown.

Leave the Chestnut Macaroons on the baking tray for a few minutes to firm up, then transfer to a wire rack to cool.

Elderflower delight

I seriously considered leaving this recipe out of the book, not because there is
anything wrong with it, but because I didn't really want you to have it. My
generous good nature has won through, however, so here it is. While I would
maintain that this is the best hedgerow delight imaginable, the Elderflowers could
easily be replaced with Japanese Rose petals. A further possibility would be to use
Rosehip Syrup (p.91) to make Turkish delight, adjusting the sugar and water
amounts accordingly.

Makes about 60 cubes

20g leaf gelatine   400ml water
20 Elderflower sprays   130g cornflour
700g granulated sugar   30g icing sugar
Juice of 2 lemons

Soak the gelatine in a shallow dish of cold water to soften. Strip the Elderflower
blossom from the stems with a fork and tie them in a piece of muslin to form a bag,
leaving a length of string. Put the granulated sugar, lemon juice and 300ml water in
a heavy-based saucepan, heat gently until the sugar is dissolved, then leave to cool.

In a bowl, mix 100g of the cornflour with the remaining 100ml water until smooth,
then stir into the lemon sugar syrup. Return the saucepan to a low heat. Squeeze the
gelatine to remove excess water, then add to the mixture and stir with a balloon
whisk until the gelatine has dissolved.

Bring the mixture very slowly to the boil and simmer for 10 minutes, stirring almost
continuously to prevent the mixture sticking and any volcanic build-up of steam.
Suspend the muslin bag of Elderflowers in the mixture and simmer, still stirring, for
a further 15 minutes, giving the muslin bag an occasional squeeze with the back of
the spoon to release the Elderflower fragrance. The mixture will gradually clarify and
become extremely gloopy. When ready, leave to cool for 10 minutes.

Mix the remaining 30g cornflour with the icing sugar. Line a shallow baking tin,
about 20cm square, with baking parchment and dust with a heaped tablespoonful
of the icing sugar and cornflour mixture. Remove the muslin bag from the gloopy
mixture, then pour it into the baking tin and place in a cool place (but not the
fridge) to set. Now refrigerate for a few hours until it becomes rubbery.

Cut the Elderflower Delight into cubes with a knife or scissors and dust with the
remaining icing sugar and cornflour.

Juniper toffee

During a visit to the Falkland Islands in 1762 a traveller, one Antoine-Joseph Pernety, spent a pleasant afternoon conversing in Latin with an unnamed friar at the local monastery. The friar helpfully passed on a large number of extraordinary remedies of the 'Take thirty-one live crayfish, caught when the moon is in Cancer' variety. Among them is a cure for 'malignant fevers', which entailed binding a live tench to each of the patient's feet for 12 hours; one for colic where the sufferer held the root of a sunflower under the armpit; and, most entertaining of all, sticking the short and curly hair of someone of the opposite sex up your nose to stop it bleeding. There are far, far worse, but I will spare you.

The one recipe which might just work – and the inspiration for my Juniper Toffee – is for '*A moift Afthma, Colds, and Diforders of the Breaft*'. A pound of crushed Juniper berries is simmered in a pound of unsalted butter for half an hour, then the berries are strained out and discarded. An equal weight of best honey is added to the remaining infused butter and the mixture put on '*an exceeding low fire till it has gained the consistency of syrup*'. My version of the recipe uses less overpowering quantities of honey and berry and makes a set toffee, not a syrup. And the flavour? Well, I absolutely love it – halfway between an English toffee and a pine wardrobe. You will need a good cooking thermometer.

Makes 1 tray

8g (about 80) Juniper berries	½ tsp cream of tartar
100g unsalted butter	A pinch of salt
350g granulated sugar	150ml water
100g honey	

Lightly butter a shallow baking tin, about 30cm square. Crush the Juniper berries and tie them in a piece of muslin to form a bag, leaving a length of string. Set aside.

Combine all the other ingredients in a heavy-based saucepan. Place over a low heat and stir frequently until the mixture comes to the boil. Turn the heat right down and hang the muslin bag over the side of the pan so it is suspended in the mixture. Continue to simmer, stirring gently and giving the bag of berries a squeeze with the spoon every minute or two. The toffee is ready when the temperature registers 137°C on a cooking thermometer, about 25 minutes after the start of cooking.

Remove the pan from the heat and put the lid on for a couple of minutes so that a little steam builds up inside (to dissolve the sugar crystals that have formed on the sides). Take off the lid and stir the toffee very gently for a few minutes as it cools a little, then pour into the prepared baking tray. Leave until set but still slightly warm. Remove from the tray (not always that easy), lay on a flat surface and score with a knife or pizza cutter into squares. Cover loosely with greaseproof paper and leave until set. When the toffee is quite cold, break it into pieces.

P.S. Toffee-making is something of a black art and there are several things that can go wrong. One of the worst problems is the butter separating out, but the pinch of salt and stirring after removal from the heat help a lot. If sugar crystals from the side of the pan make it into the finished toffee they can crystallise the whole batch (like Kurt Vonnegut's fictional *Ice Nine* does to water).

Wild flower syrup

The heady smells of May blossom – Japanese Rose, Elderflower, Hawthorn and even Dandelion – pack quite a punch, but capturing them is not that easy. Dried petals retain but a faint echo of their former glory, but syrups leave much of the perfume intact. Syrups can be used in several ways – on pancakes and ice creams, in drink mixes, or as a replacement for sugar in cakes and desserts. To make a syrup that will keep, you need to maintain a sugar concentration above 65 per cent. Boiling up blossoms in a strong sugar solution would quickly destroy the delicate aromas, but this way is gentle, if sticky.

Makes about 1 litre
Lots of freshly picked blossoms
  (about a litre)
About 1kg granulated sugar
About 550ml boiling water

Put a 2cm layer of blossoms in the bottom of a large jug, minimum 2 litres capacity. Pack the blossoms down, then sprinkle on a 1cm layer of sugar – don't worry if things all get mixed up. Continue these alternate layers of sugar and blossoms until the jug is full, keeping a note of the amount of sugar used. Cover the jug and leave to stand for 24 hours.

Empty the mixture into a saucepan and pour on 55ml of boiling water for every 100g sugar used. Heat the mixture gently, stirring, until the sugar has dissolved, then strain into a clean jug.

Pour any syrup that you are not using straight away into sterilised bottles and seal. Stored in a cool, dark cupboard, it will keep for up to a year.

Wild Strawberries
in brandy syrup

In the unlikely event that you find more Wild Strawberries than you can possibly eat fresh, it is nice to use some to make what is effectively a rumtopf. This is a powerful thing to eat on its own but goes wonderfully well with ice cream or better still, panna cotta, such as the one in my *Edible Seashore* Handbook.

Makes 1 jar
**Wild Strawberries (as many as you
  can spare)**
An equal weight of granulated sugar
Brandy

Place alternate layers of Strawberries and sugar in a sterilised jar until you reach the top. Now pour in brandy, so that the jar is brimming. You will need to have a more or less equal weight of Strawberries and sugar in the jar (though quite how you ensure this I will have to leave to you as an exercise).

Screw the lid on, shake so that any bubbles float to the top, then unscrew the lid and top up again with brandy. Gently shake occasionally and eat within a couple of months. This recipe works with any other soft wild fruit.

Dandelion jelly marmalade

This refreshing springtime marmalade is very easy to make, provided you use a good quality, sharp and unfiltered (cloudy) apple juice and jam sugar (sugar with added pectin). The colour is a lovely golden and the apple juice takes on a pleasant bitterness from the Dandelion petals.

Makes about 5 jars

1 litre good-quality sharp, fresh apple juice (do not use juice from concentrates)

80g Dandelion petals, (snip them off with scissors)

100ml freshly squeezed lemon juice (2–3 lemons)

750g jam sugar (i.e. sugar with added pectin)

Pour the apple juice into a saucepan and stir in 60g of the Dandelion petals. Bring to simmering point and remove from the heat. Cover and leave to infuse overnight.

The following day, strain the juice through a sieve to remove the petals (they will have discoloured slightly). Return the juice to the pan, add the lemon juice and heat slowly to boiling point. Add the sugar and stir until dissolved, then add the remaining dandelion petals. Increase the heat and boil rapidly for 6–7 minutes or until setting point is reached (see below).

Remove from the heat and skim the surface with a slotted spoon to remove any scum. Pour into warm sterilised jam jars, cover and seal. If you find the Dandelion petals are floating to the surface, leave until the jelly is at room temperature and then give the jar a sharp shake. You will find the petals distribute evenly throughout the setting jelly.

P.S. To test for setting, put a teaspoonful of the marmalade on to a chilled saucer. Leave for about a minute, then push the surface with your finger – if it wrinkles and the marmalade appears to be setting it is ready.

Rose jelly

The gentle native species are too light of fragrance to make this jelly so I always use the potent and heady Japanese Rose. There are many ways to do it, but this is the simplest and quickest I know. As with Dandelion Marmalade I'm using the answer to a maiden jam-maker's prayer – pectinised jam sugar – so you will not have any trouble with the set. I like Rose Jelly with a lot of flavour, so I use a lot of petals and you can up the flavour even more if you like, by hanging a muslin bag of fresh petals over the side of the pan during the last minute of cooking. Bit sticky though. And don't set fire to the muslin.

You could use Elderflowers in the same way and make Elderflower Jelly.

Makes 2 small jars

250ml water
250ml Japanese Rose petals
   (gently pressed down)

350g jam sugar (i.e. sugar with
   added pectin)
Juice of ½ lemon

Pour the water into a medium saucepan and bring to the boil. Take off the heat and stir in the petals. Pour into a bowl, cover and leave for an hour at least, or overnight if you have the time.

Strain the liquid through a fine sieve back into your pan and place over a low heat. Add the sugar and stir to dissolve, then add the lemon juice and bring to a scary, fast boil. Keep this rolling boil going for 4 minutes, then take the pan off the heat.

Allow the mixture a couple of minutes to calm down, then pour into hot sterilised jam jars, filling them to the brim before screwing on the lid.

Elderflower cordial

I have a bad habit of putting off my annual Elderflower Cordial production until mid-July and have to roam around for hours, picking a spray here and a spray there. Had I started in early June I could have picked the lot from any two trees and in a fraction of the time.

This is the best of the hedgerow soft drinks, its heady perfume an essential accompaniment to summer picnics. You should easily be able to make enough to last you the whole year, but this will be in vain if your cordial starts to go mouldy by August. There are two ways to stop this small catastrophe:

The first is to put your cordial into swing-top bottles, place the full bottles, upright, stoppers in place, into a large pan of water, carefully cover the bottle with a tea-towel to keep the hot water vapour in, and heat to about 80°C for 30 minutes. It is worth putting an old tea-towel in the saucepan first to prevent the base of the bottles overheating.

The second, much easier method is to add a Campden tablet for every 4 or 5 litres of cordial you make. The tablet should be ground up and mixed with a little water before stirring into the cordial. Campden tablets contain the preservative sulphur dioxide, which some people cannot tolerate. However, the concentration after the cordial has been diluted is tiny and considerably less than that found in many wines.

The following recipe uses a fairly high proportion of sugar, so it should last several months without either of the above treatments.

Makes about 1.8 litres

3 unwaxed lemons	2kg granulated sugar
Blossoms from 30 Elderflower heads, removed from the stems with a fork	75g citric acid – or tartaric acid, which is a little less sharp
1.3 litres water	

Cut the zest from the lemons and squeeze the juice. Put both into a large bowl and add the Elderflowers. Bring the water to the boil in a saucepan, turn off the heat and add the sugar, stirring until dissolved. Allow to cool for 10 minutes.

Pour the warm syrup over the lemon and Elderflowers and stir in the citric or tartaric acid. If you wish to use Camden tablets add half a tablet now. Cover and leave for 24 hours. Stir, then strain through a sieve lined with a sterilised muslin cloth into sterilised bottles.

Useful Things

Glossary

Alternate: Leaflets on opposite sides of a central leaf stem but in staggered positions. Compare the term 'opposite' (below).

Annual: A plant which lives for less than a year.

Axial: Arranged around a stem.

Basal: At the base of a plant – normally referring to leaves.

Biennial: A plant which grows for a year and produce flowers and fruit in the second year. Sometimes it may take three years to fruit.

Bract: A modified leaf around a flower or fruit.

Composite: A flower made up of many tiny flowers, like a daisy or dandelion.

Compound: A leaf made up of leaflets.

Leaflet: The divisions of a compound leaf.

Lobed: Divided into rounded sections.

Terminal: At the end or apex – normally of a compound leaf or a flower.

Opposite: Leaflets on opposite sides of a central leaf stem in matched pairs. Compare the term 'alternate' (above).

Perennial: A plant that lives for an indefinite length of time, but longer than one year. May flower and fruit many times.

Pinnate: A compound leaf with leaflets immediately opposite one another.

Trefoil: A leaf in three parts.

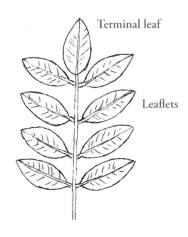

Terminal leaf

Leaflets

A compound leaf with opposite leaflets

A compound leaf with alternate leaflets

Bract

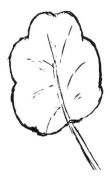

Shallowly lobed leaf

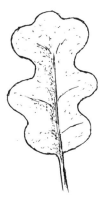

Lobed leaf

Directory

Conservation:

The four main government conservation bodies of the UK are:

Natural England
0845 600 3078
www.naturalengland.org.uk

Scottish Natural Heritage
01463 725000
www.snh.org.uk

Council for Nature Conservation and the Countryside (Northern Ireland)
02890 254835
www.cnccni.gov.uk

Countryside Council for Wales
0845 1306229
www.ccw.gov.uk

These organisations come under one unifying body:

Joint Nature Conservation Committee (JNCC)
01733 562626
www.jncc.gov.uk

Access to the countryside:

Access and several other matters of interest to the forager come under:

Department for Environment, Food and Rural Affairs (DEFRA)
0845 933 55 77
www.defra.gov.uk

The Ramblers
Defends and extends countryside access.
020 7339 8500
www.ramblers.org.uk

Societies:

Botanical Society of the British Isles
www.bsbi.org.uk

Useful reference books:

The Wild Flower Key: How to identify wild plants, trees and shrubs in Britain and Ireland (Revised Edition)
by Francis Rose and Clare O'Reilly
(Frederick Warne Publishers, 2006)

Food for Free
by Richard Mabey
(Collins new edition, 2007)

The River Cottage Preserves Handbook
by Pam Corbin (Bloomsbury, 2008)

The River Cottage Edible Seashore Handbook
by John Wright (Bloomsbury, 2009)

The River Cottage Mushroom Handbook
by John Wright (Bloomsbury, 2006)

My own website, which deals with many foraging matters is:
www.wild-food.net

For more information on identifying plants and a few extra species and recipes:
www.rivercottage.net/foraging

Acknowledgements

This is a thank you to the charming, accommodating and supremely knowledgeable people who have helped me with this book.

There are two people in particular without whom I would have thrown in the towel before I started. Bryan Edwards is the most accomplished naturalist I have ever met. I have enjoyed our many plant-hunting walks and thank him for his unflagging patience in answering my constant question: 'So what's this one called, Bryan?' The recipe section, and much else besides, owes a very great deal to my good friend Pam Corbin. Her culinary talents are legendary and I am ever thankful for the advice that she has selflessly given me.

My thanks go to Steve Alton for checking my assertions on natural history (and for finding some real howlers), to John Cockrill for his help with matters medical, to Mike Gardner for imparting his knowledge of genetics, and to Luke Hindmarsh for helping us all stay out of the magistrates' court. My thanks also to the allotment holders of Maiden Newton, for not calling the police.

My many friends at Bloomsbury have been ever helpful, ever tolerant. Many thanks to Richard Atkinson for wielding the red pen so accurately and, I am afraid, so needfully. Also to Will Webb for his sterling work on the layouts and to Janet Illsley for accomplishing her difficult task of fixing my many errors and ensuring it all looks good and makes some kind of sense. I am particularly grateful to Natalie Hunt for her steady editorial hand and for being so kind to me.

Thank you to Gordon Wise for his continuing support. Also to Rob Love and Antony Topping for having faith in my abilities and, of course, to Hugh for his terrific introduction and for inspiring me – and a whole generation.

Index

Page numbers in *italic* refer to the illustrations

access 25–8
Achillea millefolium 141, *141*
Aegopodium podagraria 100–1, *101*
Aethusa cynapium 176, *177*
Alexanders 171–2
Alliaria petiolata 42–3, *43*
Allium
  A. ursinum 144–6, *145*
  A. vineale 142–3, *143*
allotments 11–12
Alma-Tadema, Sir Lawrence 165
alternate leaflets 246, *247*
Anderson, William 81
Annual Mercury *178*, 179–80
annuals 246
Apium nodiflorum 47
apple juice
  Dandelion jelly marmalade 240, *241*
apples *see* Crab Apple
Armoracia rusticana 44–6, *45*, *46*
Artemisia absinthium 116
Arum maculatum 110, 191–3, *191–3*
Atriplex
  A. glabriuscular 60
  A. laciniata 60
  A. patula 60
  A. prostrata 60–1, *61*
Atropa belladonna 183, 186
Autumn Crocus 146
axial 246

bacon
  Hen chicken *214*, 215
Bacon, Francis 173
balsam, Himalayan 22
Barbarea 36
basal 246
Beech 16–17, 74
beef casserole with Horseradish and Chestnut
  dumplings 216, *217*
beer
  Hogweed tempura 202
berries
  berry-pickers 13–15, *14*
  poisonous 33
  see also individual types of berry
Betula
  B. pendula *158*, 159–61, *160*
  B. pubescens 161
biennials 246
Bilberry 13, 16–17, 66, *124*, 125

biodiversity 22
Birch
  Downy 161
  Silver 18–19, *158*, 159–61, *160*
    Birch Sap syrup 161
    Chestnut pancakes with Birch sap syrup 226, *227*
birds 24
biscuits
  Chestnut Florentines *228*, 229
  Chestnut macaroons *230*, 231
bistort 32
Bittercress
  Hairy 16–17, 28, 38, *39*, 63
  Large 38
  Wood 38
'Black Drop' 71
Blackberry 12, 16–17, 22, 25, 28, 29, 66–8, *67*, 137
  Bramble mousse *220*, 221
  Rosehip babas with Blackberries 224, *225*
Blackthorn 18–19, *80*, 81–2
bogs 13
Borage 16–17, 64
Boyle, Robert 17
bracts 246, *247*
Bramble 64
  Bramble mousse *220*, 221
brandy
  Wild Cherry brandy 84
  Wild Strawberries in brandy syrup *238*, 239
Brassica nigra 40–1, *41*
'bread and cheese' 73–4
Brooklime 16–17, 32, 128, *129*
Broom 16–17, 64, *65*
  Spanish 64
Bryonia dioica *194*, 195
Bryony
  Black 115, *194*, 195
  White 115, *194*, 195
Bullace 138
Bulrush 16–17, 162–5, *163*, *164*
  wild stir-fry 203
burdock 28
Butler, Dr William 92
byelaws 26

calendar, forager's 16–19
candied Primroses 64
Cardamine
  C. amara 38
  C. flexuosa 38
  C. hirsuta 38, *39*
  C. pratensis 38
Carex nigra 164
Carey, George Saville 49
Carrot, Wild 18–19, 108–9, 171–2

carrot family 33, 101, 102, 107, 108, 169, 172, 176
cars, standing on roof of 15
Castanea sativa 150, 151–2
Chaucer, Geoffrey 114
cheese
   Sorrel and Fat Hen tart 212
   Watercress omelette with cream cheese and smoked
     salmon 208, *209*
   Wild Garlic pesto 205, *205*
Chenopodium
   album 56, 57–9
   C. bonus-henricus 59
   C. rubrum 59
Cherry, Wild 12, 18–19, 83–4, *85*
   Cherry-pit 84
   Sweet Cherry Pickle 84
   Wild Cherry brandy 84
Cherry Plum 16–17, 32, 81, 138–40, *139*
Chestnut
   Horse 151
   Sweet 13, 18–19, 22, *150*, 151–2
     beef casserole with Horseradish and Chestnut
       dumplings 216, *217*
     Chestnut Florentines *228*, 229
     Chestnut macaroons *230*, 231
     Chestnut pancakes with Birch sap syrup 226, *227*
chicken, Hen *214*, 215
Chickweed, Common 11, 16–17, 52, *53*
   Chickweed pakoras *210*, 211
clothing 13
clover 62
cobnuts 147
coffee, Dandelion 137
'colonialism, environmental' 24
Comfrey 32, 189, 190
composite flowers 246
compound leaves 246, *247*
confectionery
   Elderflower delight 232, *233*
   Juniper toffee 234–5, *235*
Conium maculatum 173–5, *174–5*
Conopodium majus 104–5, *105*
conservation 22–5, 28–9
containers 13
Coombes, William 181
Corbin, Pam 66, 69, 74, 91
cordial, Elderflower 243
Corky Water-dropwort 172
Corn Salad 16–17, 130, *130*
Corylus
   C. avellana 147–9, *148*
   C. maxima 147
Countryside and Rights of Way Act (2000, CROW)
   26–8
Crab Apple 16–17, 22, 24, 26, 64, 69–71, *70–1*

Cranberry and apple tart 222, *223*
   Hawthorn and Crab Apple Leather 69–71
Cranberry 13, 16–17, 29, 126–7, *127*
   Cranberry and apple tart 222, *223*
Crataegus monogyna 72, 73–4, *74*
cream
   Bramble mousse *220*, 221
cream cheese
   Watercress omelette with cream cheese and smoked
     salmon 208, *209*
Crippen, Dr 181
Crow Garlic *see* Garlic, Crow
Cuckoo Pint 191–3
Culpeper, Nicholas 40, 55, 78, 88, 99, 104, 112,
   115, 119, 140, 175, 189
Cytisus scoparius 64, *65*

Damson 138
Dandelion 13, 16–17, 22, 28, 135–7, *136*
   Dandelion jelly marmalade 240, *241*
Datura 57
   Datura stramonium 183
Daucus carota 108–9
Delaroche, Paul 165
Dewberry 16–17, 66, 88, *88*
Digitalis purpurea 188, 189–90
Diplotaxis tenuifolia 50, *51*
Dock, Common 44, 55
Dog's Mercury 59, *178*, 179–80
dulse
   wild stir-fry 203
dumplings, Horseradish and Chestnut 216, *217*

eggs
   Watercress omelette with cream cheese and
     smoked salmon 208, *209*
Elder 12, 16–17, 22, 75, 131–3, *132*
   Elderflower cordial 243
   Elderflower delight 232, *233*
'environmental colonialism' 24
equipment 13–15, *14*
Evelyn, John 115, 152

Fasciola hepatica 47–9
Fat Hen 11, 15, 16–17, 22, 33, *56*, 57–9
   Hen chicken *214*, 215
   Sorrel and Fat Hen tart 212
Fennel 12, 16–17, 98–9, *99*
fields 13
filberts 147
Florentines, Chestnut *228*, 229
flour, Chestnut 152
flowers
   as decoration 64
   wild flower syrup *236*, 237

flukes, on Watercress 47–9
Foeniculum vulgare 98–9, *99*
Fool's Parsley 176, *177*
Fool's Watercress 47
foraging
  conservation and the law 22–9
  equipment 13–15, *14*
  when to look 15–19
Forestry Commission 26
Foxglove *188*, 189–90
Fragaria
  F. chiloensis 92
  F. moschata 93
  F. vesca 92–3, *93*
  F. virginiana 92
fruit 22–4
fungi 32

Garlic
  Crow 16–17, 142–3, *143*
    Chickweed pakoras *210*, 211
    wild stir-fry 203
  Wild (Ramsons) 18–19, 22, 63, 144–6, *145*
    Hen chicken *214*, 215
    Wild Garlic parcels 204, *204*
    Wild Garlic pesto 205, *205*
Garlic Mustard 16–17, 42–3, *43*
Gerard, John 66, 115, 119, 189
gin, Sloe 82
gloves 13
goat's cheese
  Sorrel and Fat Hen tart 212
Good King Henry 59, 60, 180
Gooseberry 12, 16–17, 94, *95*
Goosefoot 33, 57, 59, 60–1, 193
  Fig-leaved 59
  Foetid 59
  Many-seeded 59, 180
  Nettle-leaved 59
  Red 11, 18–19, 32, *58*, 59, 181, 185
  Stinking 59
Grigson, Geoffrey 73, 120
Grigson, Jane 92–3
Ground Elder 16–17, 100–1, *101*, 171–2
Ground Ivy 116

habitat loss 22
hats 13
Hawthorn 15, 16–17, 22, *72*, 73–4, *74*, 75
  Hawthorn and Crab Apple Leather 69–71
  Midland Hawthorn 73
Hazel 12, 16–17, 32, 147–9, *148*
  Chestnut Florentines *228*, 229
  Chestnut macaroons *230*, 231
  Hazelnut pastry 222

heath 13
Hemlock 108, 117, 173–5, *174–5*
Hemlock Water-dropwort 33, 46, 169, *170*, 171–2
Hen chicken *214*, 215
Henbane 181–3, *182*
Heracleum sphondylium 102, *103*
Herrick, Robert 84, 93
Himalayan balsam 22
Hippophae rhamnoides 156, *157*
Hogweed 16–17, 102, *103*, 171–2
  Hogweed tempura 202
Hop 16–17, 115–16, *116*
Horehound 116
Horse Chestnut 151
Horseradish 16–17, 44–6, *45*, *46*
  beef casserole with Horseradish and Chestnut
    dumplings 216, *217*
Humulus lupulus 115–16, *116*
Hyoscyamus niger 181–3, *182*

identifying plants 32–3

jelly
  Dandelion jelly marmalade 240, *241*
  Elderflower jelly 242
  Redcurrant jelly 97
  Rose jelly 242
Jelly Ears
  wild stir-fry 203
Jimson Weed 183
Johns, Reverend 38
Juniper 18–19, 29, 153–5, *154*, 197
  Juniper pot 213
  Juniper toffee 234–5, *235*
Juniperus communis 153–5, *154*

knives 13, 29
knotweed, Japanese 22

Lady's Smock 38
Lamb's Lettuce 130
laws 13, 15, 25–9
leaflets 246, *247*
leaves
  edible tree leaves 74
  shapes *247*
legislation 13, 15, 25–9
Lémery, Louis 123
lemon
  Watermint sorbet *218*, 219
lily of the valley 146
Lime 18–19, 74
lobed leaves 246, *247*
Loco Weed 183
Lords and Ladies 110, 146, 191–3, *191–3*

Mabey, Richard 32, 66, 73, 88, 152, 165
macaroons, Chestnut *230*, 231
Mallow, Common 16–17, *54*, 55, 114
Malus sylvestris 69–71, *70–1*
Malva sylvestris 54, 55
Manning, Anne 42
Maple, Field 161
Marjoram, Wild 18–19, *122*, 123
marmalade, Dandelion jelly 240, *241*
May blossom *72*, 73
meadows 13
Mentha
  M. aquatica 117–19, *118*
  M. arvensis 120
  M. spicata 120, *121*
  M. suaveolens 120, *121*
Mercurialis
  M. annua 178, 179–80
  M. perennis 178, 179–80
Mercury
  Annual *178*, 179–80
  Dog's 59, *178*, 179–80
Mint
  Corn 120
  Round-leaved 18–19, 120, *121*
  Spearmint 18–19, 120, *121*
  Watermint 13, 18–19, 25, 117–19, *118*
    Watermint sorbet *218*, 219
mousse, Bramble *220*, 221
Mugwort 116
mushrooms 32
Mustard, Black 16–17, 40–1, *41*
Myrrhis odorata 106, 107

National Trust 24, 26
Natural England 29
Nettle, Stinging 12, 18–19, 22, 32, 55, 112–14, *113*
  Nettle ravioli 206–7, *207*
  Nettle soup *200*, 201
Nightshade
  Black 32, 33, 57, 60, *184*, 185
  Deadly 169, 171, 183, 186
  Woody 186, *187*
nightshade family 59, 60, 181

Oak 74
Oenanthe
  O. crocata 170, 171–2
  O. pimpinelloides 172
omelette
  Watercress omelette with cream cheese and smoked salmon 208, *209*
opposite leaflets 246, *247*
Orache
  Babington's 60

Common 60
Frosted 60
Spear-leaved 11, 18–19, 60–1, *61*
Origanum
  O. majorana 123
  O. onites 123
  O. vulgare 122, 123
Oxalis
  O. acetosella 62–3, *63*
  O. corniculata 62

pakoras, Chickweed *210*, 211
pancakes
  Chestnut pancakes with Birch sap syrup 226, *227*
Papaver
  P. rhoeas 34, 35
  P. somniferum 35
parasites, flukes 47–9
Parsnip, Wild 18–19, 108, *109*, 171–2
pasta
  Nettle ravioli 206–7, *207*
Pastinaca sativa 108, *109*
pastry, Hazelnut 222
pepper dulse
  wild stir-fry 203
perennials 246
Perennial Wall Rocket 12, 18–19, 32, 50, *51*
pesto, Wild Garlic 205, *205*
pickers *14*, 15
Pignut 13, 18–19, 104–5, *105*
  Nettle ravioli 206–7, *207*
  Wild Garlic pesto 205, *205*
Pine, Scots 197
pinnate leaves 246
Plantlife 24
Pliny the Elder 87, 181
Plum
  Cherry 16–17, 32, 81, 138–40, *139*
  Wild 18–19, 138–40, *139*
poisonous plants 32–3, 166–97
pollution 12
Polygonaceae 110
Poppy
  Common 16–17, *34*, 35
  Opium 35
pork
  Juniper pot 213
potato family 33, 169
Potentilla anserina 78, *79*
Primrose 64
private land 25–6
Prunus
  P. avium 83–4, *85*
  P. cerasifera 138–40, *139*
  P. domestica 138–40, *139*
  P. spinosa 80, 81–2

Ramsons *see* Garlic, Wild
Randolph, Mary 119
rare plants 28
Raspberry 18–19, 32, 66, *86*, 87–8
ravioli, Nettle 206–7, *207*
Redcurrant 12, 15, 18–19, 66, *96*, 97
Reedmace 16–17, 162–5, *163*, *164*
    wild stir-fry 203
Ribes
    R. rubrum 96, 97
    R. uva-crispa 94, *95*
rice
    Wild Garlic parcels 204, *204*
Rocket, Perennial Wall 12, 18–19, 32, 50, *51*
Rorippa nasturtium-aquaticum 47–9, *48*
Rosa
    R. arvensis 89–91, *90*
    R. canina 89–91, *90*
    R. rugosa 90, 91
Rosaceae 81
Rose 64
    Dog 18–19, 89–91, *90*
    Field 16–17
    Japanese 16–17, *90*, 91
        Rose jelly 242
rose family 81
Rosehips 90–1, *90*
    Chestnut Florentines *228*, 229
    Rosehip babas with Blackberries 224, *225*
    Rosehip syrup 91
Rowan 12, 18–19, 75–7, *75*, *76*, 133
Rubus
    R. caesius 88, *88*
    R. fruticosus 66–8, *67*
    R. idaeus 86, 87–8
rum
    Rosehip babas with Blackberries 224, *225*
Rumex
    R. acetosa 110–11, *111*
    R. acetosella 111

safety 13, 32
Sambucus nigra 131–4, *132*, *134*
Samphire, Marsh 25, 28
sausage meat
    Wild Garlic parcels 204, *204*
'schedule 8' list 28
scissors 13
Scotland, right to roam 25
Scurvygrasses 38
Sea Beet 22
    wild stir-fry 203
Sea Buckthorn 12, 18–19, 156, *157*
seaside 13
Sedge, Common 164
Sheep's Sorrel 18–19

Silverweed 18–19, 78, *79*
Silvester, Rev. Tipping 112
Sites of Special Scientific Interest (SSSIs) 28–9
Sloe 18–19, 22, 29, *80*, 81–2
    Sloe Gin 82
smoked salmon
    Watercress omelette with cream cheese
        and smoked salmon 208, *209*
Solanaceae 57, 60, 169, 181
Solanum
    S. dulcamara 186, *187*
    S. nigrum 184, 185
sorbet, Watermint *218*, 219
Sorbus aucuparia 75–7, *75*, *76*
Sorrel
    Common Sorrel 13, 16–17, 22, 29, 110–11, *111*,
        193
        Sorrel and Fat Hen tart 212
    Procumbent Yellow Sorrel 62
    Sheep's Sorrel 18–19, 111
    Wood Sorrel 13, 22, 62–3, *63*
soup, Nettle *200*, 201
Spartium junceum 64
Spearmint 18–19, 120, *121*
Stace, Clive 61
Stellaria
    S. holostea 52, *53*
    S. media 52, *53*
Stinging Nettle *see* Nettle, Stinging
Stitchwort, Greater 52, *53*
Storck, Dr 17
Strangford Lough 26
Strawberry
    Alpine 92
    Chilean 92
    Hautbois 93
    Virginian 92
    Wild 12, 15, 18–19, 66, 92–3, *93*
        Wild Strawberries in brandy syrup *238*, 239
streams 13
Sweet Cicely 18–19, 22, *106*, 107
Sweet Gale 116
Sycamore 161
Symphytum 190
syrup
    Birch sap syrup 161
    Rosehip syrup 91
    wild flower syrup *236*, 237

Tamus communis 194, 195
tansy 32, 78
Taraxacum 135–7, *136*
tarts
    Blackberry or Bilberry tart 222
    Cranberry and apple tart 222, *223*
    Sorrel and Fat Hen tart 212

Taxus baccata 196, 197
tempura, Hogweed 202
terminal 246
Theft Act (1968) 26, 77
Thorn Apple 183
toffee, Juniper 234–5, *235*
trespassing 25–8
Typha latifolia 162–5, *163*, *164*

Umbelliferaceae 169, 172
urban foraging 12
Urtica dioica 112–14, *113*

Vaccinium
  V. macrocarpon 126
  V. myrtillus 124, 125
  V. oxycoccos 126–7, *127*
Valerianella locusta 130, *130*
verjuice 69
Veronica beccabunga 128, *129*
Violet, Sweet 64

Wall Rocket, Perennial 12, 18–19, 32, 50,
  51
Walnut 161

Warren, Piers 112
Water-dropwort
  Corky 172
  Hemlock 33, 46, 169, *170*, 171–2
Watercress 13, 15, 18–19, 25, 47–9, *48*
  Watercress omelette with cream cheese and smoked
    salmon 208, *209*
Watermint 13, 18–19, 25, 117–19, *118*
  Watermint sorbet *218*, 219
Whitebeam 77
wild boar 105
wild flower syrup *236*, 237
wild stir-fry 203
Wildlife and Countryside Act (1981) 28
Wildlife Trust 26
Wintercress 13, 18–19
  American 36, *37*
  Common 36
Withering, William 189, 190
wood, cherry 84
woodlands 12, 13
Wormwood 116

Yarrow 18–19, 32, 116, 141, *141*
Yew *196*, 197

River Cottage Handbooks

River Cottage Handbook No.1

Mushrooms
by John Wright
introduced by Hugh Fearnley-Whittingstall

River Cottage Handbook No.2

Preserves
by Pam Corbin
introduced by Hugh Fearnley-Whittingstall

River Cottage Handbook No.3

Bread
by Daniel Stevens
introduced by Hugh Fearnley-Whittingstall

River Cottage Handbook No.4

Veg Patch
by Mark Diacono
introduced by Hugh Fearnley-Whittingstall

River Cottage Handbook No.5

Edible Seashore
by John Wright
introduced by Hugh Fearnley-Whittingstall

River Cottage Handbook No.6

Sea Fishing
by Nick Fisher
introduced by Hugh Fearnley-Whittingstall

River Cottage Handbook No.7

Hedgerow
by John Wright
introduced by Hugh Fearnley-Whittingstall

River Cottage Handbook No.8

Cakes
by Pam Corbin
introduced by Hugh Fearnley-Whittingstall

River Cottage Handbook No.9

Fruit
by Mark Diacono
introduced by Hugh Fearnley-Whittingstall

River Cottage Handbook No.10

Herbs
by Nikki Duffy
introduced by Hugh Fearnley-Whittingstall

River Cottage Handbook No.11

Chicken & Eggs
by Mark Diacono
introduced by Hugh Fearnley-Whittingstall

River Cottage Handbook No.12

Booze
by John Wright
introduced by Hugh Fearnley-Whittingstall

Seasonal, Local, Organic, Wild

FOR FURTHER INFORMATION AND
TO ORDER ONLINE, VISIT
WWW.RIVERCOTTAGE.NET